AGILE MINDSET Ma.g.i.c.

STORIES FROM THE TRENCHES

YASHASREE BARVE

INDIA • SINGAPORE • MALAYSIA

Notion Press

No.8, 3rd Cross Street,
CIT Colony, Mylapore,
Chennai, Tamil Nadu – 600004

First Published by Notion Press 2020
Copyright © Yashasree Barve 2020
All Rights Reserved.

ISBN 978-1-63606-713-1

This book has been published with all efforts taken to make the material error-free after the consent of the author. However, the author and the publisher do not assume and hereby disclaim any liability to any party for any loss, damage, or disruption caused by errors or omissions, whether such errors or omissions result from negligence, accident, or any other cause.

While every effort has been made to avoid any mistake or omission, this publication is being sold on the condition and understanding that neither the author nor the publishers or printers would be liable in any manner to any person by reason of any mistake or omission in this publication or for any action taken or omitted to be taken or advice rendered or accepted on the basis of this work. For any defect in printing or binding the publishers will be liable only to replace the defective copy by another copy of this work then available.

CONTENTS

About This Book   7

How to Read This Book?   9

Acknowledgements   11

About The Author   13

Introduction   15

    Agile Mindset – The Why Before What and How   17

    Musings About Mindsets   23

    Back to the Basics   29

    Let the Magic Begin   35

PART 1   39

    Transparency   41

    Openness   49

    Courage   55

    Feedback culture   63

    Measure What Matters   69

PART 2 — 75

- Collaboration — 77
- Self-organisation — 83
- Psychological Safety — 89
- Trust — 97
- Collective Ownership — 103
- Respect — 109
- Commitment — 115
- Life Without Project Managers — 123
- Empowerment — 129
- Gemba — 135
- Customer Centricity — 141
- Working With Business — 147

PART 3 — 153

- Inspect and Adapt — 155
- Focus - Being Present — 163
- Timeboxing — 169
- Cadence — 175
- Simplicity — 181
- Prioritisation — 187

PART 4 — 193

    Continuous Improvement — 195

    Excellence — 203

    Sustainable Development — 209

References — *215*

Image Credits — *217*

ABOUT THIS BOOK

Welcome to the book 'Agile Mindset Ma.g.i.c, Stories from the trenches.' This is my honest rendition of what I have experienced over years of practising agile methods and coaching agile teams.

I have been authoring this book iteratively and incrementally over two years now. I wrote the book in small chunks jotting about all the things I found noteworthy from an agile mindset perspective. Later, I started blogging on LinkedIn on agile mindset and received feedback from agile enthusiasts.

This book is a collection of several blogs knitted together as a book. Four themes emerged out of the blogs as I brought it all together. The focus of the book is on those four themes with a deep dive into each along with examples. The 'Stories from the trenches' part is about my experience of what worked and what did not about that particular aspect of the mindset. I have also included techniques that clicked, which may be helpful to you along with additional reading on the topic.

If you are an agile coach, a scrum master, a leader or a manager who is looking at instilling an agile mindset in your teams or taking your teams to the next level, this book is for you.

HOW TO READ THIS BOOK?

Short answer:

Either 'start to finish' as you would read a novel or simply open a page and begin reading from anywhere you like.

Long answer:

If you don't like reading long books and would instead prefer reading short articles, then you can randomly go through any page in this book and read, as most of the chapters are short.

If you are someone like me who likes to read books from the first page to the last, you will discover a simple structure that groups related concepts together.

I sincerely hope you enjoy reading this book and that it helps in the agile journey for you, your teams and organisations.

ACKNOWLEDGEMENTS

Authoring this book has been my dream for several years, and many people have helped me in turning this into reality.

Acknowledgements have to start with my family. Thanks to my husband, Mr. Parag Shridhar Barve, who has always been there to encourage me, and for creating time and space for me to take up this huge task. Thanks to my children, Kaustubh and Gauri who take pride in their mother's endeavours and keep motivating me.

Thanks to my parents Mr. Bhalchandra Kulkarni and Mrs. Arundhati Kulkarni, my foundational support, for reminding me of a little bit of the writing I used to do as a child as well as waking up the writer in me that was asleep. Thanks to my late mother in law, Mrs. Priya Shridhar Barve for her continuous support. My entire extended family has been a tremendous moral support and counsellor to keep lifting my spirits up.

Thanks to my sisters at my workplace, Priti Vyas, Vidya Sridharan, Srilakshmibala Prakhya and Sirisha Pera for nudging me to finish this book. Special thanks to Priti and Vidya for providing valuable comments for making this book better, it means a lot to me.

My agile learning journey has been full of learning from several people from my organisation, Tata Consultancy Services, as well as from several customers. Thanks to all my fellow *agilists* from Tata Consultancy Services for giving the push to my agile journey and co-creating several stories in the professional life that I have penned in this book.

Thanks to my leaders at Tata Consultancy Services, especially the Corporate Agile Initiative Team as well as the HiTech Unit Leadership for enabling me with the right empowerment, opportunities and wide exposure.

I would like to thank the exceptional scrum masters and coaches at the Gurgaon Agile chapter. I have learned a lot from each one of you, and that has helped me shape this book better.

Thanks to the team at Notion Press, who helped me in refining the content and for coming up with this beautiful design to give the book a great look. Thanks to Pixabay for the beautiful images as well as the Geek and Poke Cartoon series for helping me break the monotony.

My acknowledgement would not be complete without thanking the inspiring agile community and the thought leaders through whose books and other works I have learned the agile ways of working. I am grateful to be a part of a community that thrives on helping each other for their betterment and growth.

ABOUT THE AUTHOR

Yashasree Barve is an Agile Coach and Transformation Consultant at Tata Consultancy Services (TCS). She has been working in the Information Technology industry since 1998, delivering enterprise solutions across the breadth of the technology landscape. Her work includes transformation consulting and coaching for customers and teams to help embrace the agile ways of working.

As a practitioner of agile methods since 2007, she has enjoyed the agile way of working as a scrum team member (a technical architect), a scrum master and an agile coach.

She is a Certified Scrum Master, Certified Scrum Professional, Professional Scrum Master (PSM1) and a Scaled Agile Program Consultant (SPC 5). As an SPC, she has trained over 350 TCS associates and customer employees for SAFe Agilist, SAFe Practitioner, and the SAFe Scrum Master Certification programs through several training sessions.

Yashasree has been a contributor in an organisation-wide agile initiative since 2013 and has been sharing her experience and expertise in the agile ways of working with various customer stakeholders of her organisation. In 2017, TCS awarded her with the 'Top Individual Agile' contributor award.

She has worked as the Unit Agile Leader for the HiTech Business unit of TCS since 2015. In this role, she has coached and trained hundreds of teams as well as consulted several customers on agile transformation across the unit.

As an avid blogger and conference speaker, she has spoken at several conferences such as Agile India, Agile Tour India, RubyConf India, Agile in Business, Regional Scrum Gatherings and Women in Agile. She is also a co-founder of an agile conference 'TCS Agile Café' internal to TCS to 'Network-Learn-Inspire' and has organised the same for five years successfully across various locations in India in the TCS offices during 2013-18.

At work, she actively contributes to the 'Diversity and Inclusion' initiative through a 'Circle of Women' initiative that is aimed at 'Professional Development for women at the workplace.' She also contributes to various community welfare initiatives through 'Sankalp—a promise to make a difference' in the areas of health, environment and education.

She is a wife to Parag and a mother to two wonderful kids, Kaustubh and Gauri. Yashasree considers her family to be the foundational support to everything that she does. She loves to read, sing, listen to music and go on walks.

INTRODUCTION

Agile mindset is a topic close to the heart of many in the field of agile coaching, be it a scrum master, an agile coach or leaders, especially in the digital or transformation space.

In the year 2007, I was working as a technologist on a customer project, which was when I became aware of the agile ways of working. I got fascinated as I read about the agile manifesto, scrum and extreme programming, and applied the same in my project. As my teams and I got better at the ways of working by continually inspecting and adapting, I thoroughly enjoyed the way we worked. We churned out unique products while building excellent teams.

I loved sharing my experience of how the agile methods helped us progress towards excellence in software development at my organisation, Tata Consultancy Services (TCS). By 2011, I had turned into a storyteller! Since then I have enjoyed hundreds of interactions with various customer stakeholders, right from the architects to the project managers, directors of application development, support, infrastructure to the CxO level and the fortune 500 customers of TCS.

These interactions brought out several interesting aspects of their challenges in embracing the agile methods. They were intrigued about the ways to bring in the mindset change, as the training sessions mostly focused on the practices. They wanted to know how to engage effectively with their teams embarking on the agile journey and help them navigate the 'why' and 'how' of the mindset change.

I have since then conducted several workshops with teams focused on the most significant barrier the 'mindset change.' Everything else falls in place post addressing this barrier.

This book consolidates my experience in interacting with customer stakeholders, business stakeholders, leaders and teams, and addressing their concerns and questions regarding agile methods as well as the mindset. I hope that the coaches and leaders helping teams and organisations embracing agility would find this narration from the trenches useful.

AGILE MINDSET – THE WHY BEFORE WHAT AND HOW

AGILE MINDSET – THE WHY BEFORE WHAT AND HOW

"Learn from yesterday, live for today, hope for tomorrow. The important thing is not to stop questioning."

– Albert Einstein

Not long ago, enterprises developed software in a yearly or a multi-year release schedule with elaborate planning and tracking of the plan. There were delays throughout the schedule due to various reasons. Business stakeholders suggested major changes during the 'User Acceptance Testing' or the UAT phase, thus resulting in unpleasant discussions.

While the development team claimed the proposed changes were a new requirement or an enhancement, the business claimed that it was a failure to capture the requirements correctly or that it was an implicit requirement. The heated debates would only be a 'lose-lose' for the business as well as for the development teams. Long discussions on perfecting the art of capturing requirements never led to any meaningful outcomes.

WATERFALL JOKES

The major shift in thinking started when the tsunami of digital technologies took the world by its storm. Digital native companies like Amazon, Facebook, Google and several others brought new ideas, features and products to the market quickly. The speed at which these companies rolled out new features was maddening for the enterprises that were still reeling under long development cycles.

People within the enterprises could see the difference in agility between the consumer apps they loved to use and the enterprise apps they had to use. This forced the leaders in enterprises and the business stakeholders to rethink their ways of working.

To add to that, the **volatile, uncertain, complex and ambiguous** nature of today brought its challenges. The uncertainty of new technologies and trends increased the anxiety about investments.

The response to these issues demanded **communication, collaboration and a different style of leadership that embraced problem-solving and critical thinking.** To be always ready for ambiguity, analyse and serve the needs as they arise was the key. That is where agile came in.

This change in the thinking of organisations in terms of embracing agility today is evident. The CxO and business conversations have changed from "why should we embrace agile ways?" or "will it work here?" to "how do we embrace agility?"

With this context set on 'why,' let us now dive deeper into 'what' and 'how' of the agile ballgame.

MUSINGS ABOUT MINDSETS

MUSINGS ABOUT MINDSETS

"Unless someone like you cares a whole awful lot, nothing is going to get better. It's not."

– Dr. Seuss

As I meet teams, managers, business or leaders on their journey of agile ways of working, I often hear that the real challenge to bring about the change is not learning the process, practices or techniques but changing **'the mindset.'**

As per the Oxford dictionary, the word mindset means "a set of attitudes or fixed ideas that someone has, and that is often difficult to change." 'The mind being set' sounds like set in stone and hard to change.

While there are several theories around mindsets, I find the 'Growth Mindset' concept impressive as described in the book "Mindset: The New Psychology of Success" by Carol Dweck. The growth mindset believes that intelligence can be developed leading to the desire to learn and therefore a tendency to embrace challenges, persist in the face of setbacks, see efforts as a path of mastery and learn from criticism. It also believes in finding lessons and inspiration in the success of others, helping reach ever-higher levels of achievement, giving a greater sense of free will.

I believe that one can learn and instil the new ways of working, including the agile mindset. The agile mindset also complements the growth mindset concept very well.

Mindsets are typically driven or formed by our values, thoughts, habits, experiences along with what we have heard or seen working in our work, life or elsewhere. Depending upon the diversity of exposure, learning from a wider audience and hearing from the experience of others can make one relook at their thought process as well as their mindset.

An agile mindset is an agile way of thinking that translates into an agile way of working. It may mean different things to people depending upon their roles or personas. For a software development team, it may mean responding quickly to change while for a business, it may mean treating the features as a hypothesis and changing those based upon the user feedback.

For IT operations, it may mean visualizing work in progress to maximize the flow. In contrast, for business operations, it may mean as a value stream mapping in the process of identifying and eliminating waste, bringing efficiency and flexibility.

The first step to bring the agile mindset is to find out what agility means to individuals, teams and stakeholders. The second step would be to introduce relevant experiences or discuss different approaches for problem-solving.

In this book, I will take you through how an agile mindset can be amplified through an agile way of working in software development, especially scrum. Basic exposure to the agile manifesto and scrum would help understand the concepts elaborated in this book.

BACK TO THE BASICS

BACK TO THE BASICS

"An investment in knowledge always pays the best interest."

– Benjamin Franklin

Before we begin looking at the concepts of the agile mindset, let us revisit the basics.

To understand the agile mindset, one needs to start understanding three things, one—the agile manifesto values, two—the agile manifesto principles and three—the scrum guide.

The 'Agile Manifesto' values are the closest to my heart. The agile manifesto emphasises individuals and their interactions, customer collaboration and responding to change to ensure that the working software caters to what customers need.

Manifesto for Agile Software Development

We are uncovering better ways of developing software by doing it and helping others to do the same. Through this work, we have come to value:

- Individuals and interactions over processes and tools.
- Working software over comprehensive documentation.
- Customer collaboration over contract negotiation.
- Responding to change over following a plan.

That is, while there is value in the items on the right, we value the items on the left more.

The agile manifesto brings twelve principles that talk about customer satisfaction through continuous or frequent delivery of valuable software in a shorter timescale while welcoming changing requirements and embracing simplicity. It promotes teams of motivated individuals who get the right support to self-organise, focus on technical excellence, interact with business effectively face to face and deliver at a sustainable pace while reflecting on being better. This is indeed a different human-centric, lightweight, iterative and an incremental way of working that builds 'responding to change' into the DNA of the team.

Principles behind the Agile Manifesto

We follow these principles:

1. Our highest priority is to satisfy the customer through early and continuous delivery of valuable software.

2. Welcome changing requirements, even late in development. Agile processes harness change for the customer's competitive advantage.

3. Deliver working software frequently, from a couple of weeks to a couple of months, with a preference to the shorter timescale.

4. Business people and developers must work together daily throughout the project.

5. Build projects around motivated individuals by providing them with the environment and support they need and trust them to get the job done.

6. The most efficient and effective method of conveying information to and within a development team is face-to-face conversation.

7. Working software is the primary measure of progress.

8. Agile processes promote sustainable development. The sponsors, developers and users should be able to maintain a constant pace indefinitely.

9. Continuous attention to technical excellence and good design enhances agility.

10. Simplicity—the art of maximising the amount of work not done is essential.

11. The best architectures, requirements and designs emerge from self-organising teams.

12. At regular intervals, the team reflects on how to become more effective, then tunes and adjusts its behaviour accordingly.

While agile manifesto is at a conceptual level, the scrum framework suggests essential practices. Scrum is a lightweight yet powerful set of values, principles and practices. The scrum guide is short but has compelling content that has inspired thousands to experiment with its framework for developing, delivering and sustaining complex products.

Scrum has three pillars of 'Transparency, Inspection and Adaptation,' and five core values of 'Focus, Openness, Respect, Courage and Commitment.' Scrum has three roles (scrum master, product owner and team) and five events (sprint planning, daily sync up, sprint review, sprint retrospective and sprint) to help the team deliver value using the three artefacts—product backlog, sprint backlog and increment.

These three lighthouses influence most of the concepts, practices and techniques in this book. I also believe that the lean concepts that focus on maximizing customer value while minimizing waste are immensely helpful. While teams use agile ways, they often find it useful to complement it with lean concepts like flow, continuous improvement and value along with techniques like Kanban, value stream mapping and visualization.

LET THE MAGIC BEGIN

It is easier to start by learning the practices, techniques and the new language. This gives the teams a good start in adopting a new way of working. However, it may not be enough to sustain the change. No real progress or value creation happens through the mechanics of practices without the right mindset.

The mindset change is also the hardest thing to do; however, small changes in thinking move the needle slowly towards the goal. The agile-scrum values and principles guide the teams like a 'North Star,' as they transform their ways of working. Magical things happen when teams see those "Aha" moments when they realize the power of the agile values and principles to achieve the right business outcomes.

I have consolidated my thoughts around the agile mindset into an acronym, 'Ma.g.i.c.' I love acronyms that make important things stay with us for a longer time. It helped me during my academics. I loved it when I saw it in books and movies; including my favourite 'Avengers' using EDITH abbreviated for Even Dead I'm The Hero.

Ma.g.i.c stands for 'Making it transparent,' 'genuinely collaborate,' inspect, adapt and continuously improve.

My understanding of bringing in an agile mindset fold into this magic formula in this book will take you through each of these elements one by one.

So get ready to witness the **Ma.g.i.c.**

Ma – **Ma**ke it transparent

G – **G**enuinely collaborate

I – **I**nspect and adapt

C – **C**ontinuously improve

PART 1

Ma	Make it transparent
G	Genuinely collaborate
I	Inspect and adapt
C	Continuously improve

TRANSPARENCY

TRANSPARENCY

"The single most important ingredient of success is transparency because transparency builds Trust."

– Denise Morrison

Transparency, a scrum pillar, acts as a foundation for instilling agile behaviours. Transparency is about making information about progress and impediments readily available to all stakeholders. Radiating the information to whomever it may concern yields transparency. Visualisation brings in many advantages as the human brain processes visuals much more easily than text. The information radiators could be on walls with sticky notes in a Kanban board, on big screens in the team area or even on everyone's desktops or laptops, acting as a guiding force on a day-to-day basis.

The artefact transparency ensures that the product backlog, sprint backlog and the progress made in creating the increments are visible to everyone. This helps the team to focus and get things done. The team does not need to 'report back' through fancy weekly status reports, as the progress is available for the stakeholders to see in real-time. It cuts down the waste in the process. A living and updated product backlog also make the product roadmap visible to the team.

Scrum events help to surface the team's progress or any impediments. The sprint planning ensures that everyone understands the work items in the upcoming sprint. And, the sprint review ensures that the progress made is transparent to everyone. The daily sync up ensures that the team flags any impediments as well as shares their daily progress to self-organise, by bringing everyone on the same page. Meanwhile, retrospective ensures that everyone brings their inputs to improve the ways of working to the table, and understands how the action items progress to make things better.

Being transparent is not easy; it takes courage. Teams also need to feel safe to make the progress of their work and the impediments visible to all stakeholders. The leaders need to assure them that the information would help, and in turn, not punish the team. Irrespective of the tools used or techniques applied, transparency works only when the team members raise the right flags at the right time without any hesitation.

TRANSPARENCY IN POST 2.0

WHY POLITICIANS LIKE TWITTER

Teams that send out a weekly report of the sprint progress can instead make their sprint dashboards transparent in real-time. Apart from saving time, this will prevent the team from getting into the trap of painting an 'all is well' picture in reports. Managers should not use these dashboards to track and control the deviations. Teams can use those to self-organise. Also, teams can log and track the impediments so that those do not become a hindrance to achieving the sprint goal.

Transparency helps to build trust and safety. It helps in inspecting and adapting as well. It also helps the leaders move from command and control towards participatory leadership styles. Openness, courage, feedback culture and the right metrics set the tone for transparency in agile teams.

Stories from the trenches

Here is a story about a group of agile teams that have used agile practices to deliver working software to their business stakeholders. They valued transparency in the agile way of working and extended that to their life outside of the project work.

They called it 'ADC Live,' where ADC referred to the Agile Development Center. A wall was set up inside the work location, inviting ideas to make the work environment better. Team members put their ideas transparently on the wall using sticky notes. Then the members selected a few ideas for implementing them through voting.

Another wall was set up to track the implementation of the selected ideas. People who volunteered to implement created relevant stories on sticky notes and worked on those in sprints. A lot of interesting things were driven through this initiative, such as a weekly knowledge sharing session on the floor, creating a stress buster room, an open for all library through the donation of old books, 10 minutes of Monday motivation TED talks, inspiring people to stay hydrated and much more.

Transparency played a significant role in driving pull-based participation, inspiring people and urging them to make a difference.

Read, Explore, Evolve

The product backlog and the sprint backlog has to be transparent to the scrum team (product owner, scrum master and the development team), and also to the stakeholders, such as any leadership that must know the progress to plan budgets or roadmaps and business stakeholders who need to know the progress of features and so on.

Co-located teams often use sticky notes on the walls to manage their backlog of work. However, this may create a disadvantage to some, like team members who have to work remotely for some reason. Members who need to work remotely may struggle to keep up with what is going on. While physical boards work great, one should ensure the transparency is available to everyone equally.

Digital Kanban boards proved to be a boon when the teams had to work remotely in an emergency, such as the lockdown imposed by Covid-19. Always enabling teams with digital tools irrespective of the co-location, keeps them ready for any new normal that may emerge.

When the team co-creates the list of artefacts or metrics they would like to make visible, it establishes the much-needed pull.

Team members who hesitate in being transparent or bringing up issues often stall the progress. Bringing up the issues for discussion to resolve any impediments in attaining transparency would be helpful.

OPENNESS

OPENNESS

"The mind is like a parachute, it doesn't work unless it is open."

———◆———

Openness, one of the essential scrum values, is critical in bringing transparency to work. The scrum guide says, "the Scrum Team and its stakeholders agree to be open about all the work and the challenges with performing the work."

One of the stories I had read in my childhood had the protagonist say "Open Sesame" to open the cave full of treasure. I believe that openness is also a key to open up the treasure of being an incredible member of the scrum team.

The agile team and its stakeholders need to be open in many different ways. During conversations about the requirements or stories, the team members should ask all the questions they have, and the business stakeholders should share the relevant information. This openness prevents back and forth communication during the sprint.

While estimating the stories, the team members should speak up their perspectives or risks they see. They need not worry about what others, especially the senior team members, may think about it. Different opinions often strengthen the shared understanding of the requirements, paving the way for a shared commitment to estimation.

During the daily stand up, team members should openly share the real status of their stories or tasks, raising an early flag for risks and impediments. This helps in self-organisation and achieving sprint outcomes.

During sprint reviews, team members should be open to demonstrate the actual progress on the work that they have done. Similarly, the stakeholders should be open to listen to the team's views and provide constructive feedback that can make the product better.

During sprint retrospective, nothing more matters than openness. The retrospective helps to look back at what went well and what did not. Open and honest feedback from the team members makes it effective.

Being open helps to surface issues and impediments. It takes time to open up with the team through slowly building trust and psychological safety within.

Stories from the trenches

Here are some stories from my experience where lack of openness created problems.

There was a scrum team comprising of team members as well as their supervisors who were working together. This turned out to be an inhibition for team members to be open up. The team members hesitated to bring up their issues in front of their supervisors during the Scrum events, as they felt it would affect their performance management. They had a feeling that asking questions or seeking help from others may look like being unskilled, thus leading to poor performance ratings.

The team members also hesitated to contest views expressed by their supervisors in meetings, such as estimation or sprint planning. They simply agreed to what the supervisors had to say.

This lack of openness led to many issues like the real problems not surfacing until the last moment. The team members often struggled to complete the tasks where there was ambiguity, as they were afraid to ask questions or call for help. This often led to the failing of sprint commitments.

Dealing with this issue was a major problem as moving the supervisors out of the scrum team was not a practical option. We had to work with the supervisors to bring in safety in the minds of the team members.

Another team failed to bring in openness due to office politics. The team had people whose agenda was different from the team's agenda. This created a massive hindrance for welcoming openness.

We addressed this by bringing in alignment with the supervisors about the team's goals or working with influential leaders who can coach and mentor the people. Only if the leaders make it a priority and spend time with people about being open, there is a hope of bringing openness.

Read, Explore, Evolve

One way to address the openness issue is to ensure no appraiser-appraisee relationship exists in one team. However, that may not always be possible due to the limitations of the organizational design, talent availability or such.

Another way is to coach the supervisor on the value of openness and take the help of the supervisor to open up the team members. This has worked well for me in one team.

One may also want to consider taking the help of an influential leader to discuss how openness is important and helpful to the organization.

Bringing up the topic of openness and encouraging the team to include it in team norms could also be a good first step. When the team members' expectations are set about being open, it naturally helps them set the tone for open conversations.

COURAGE

COURAGE

"It takes courage to grow up and become who you are."

– e. e. cummings

Courage is a scrum value that complements openness to bring in transparency. The scrum guide defines courage as in 'the Scrum Team members have the courage to do the right thing and work on tough problems.'

Traditionally, the project team members may not be used to speaking their minds. The tech leads or project managers would take the majority of the decisions and expect the team members to deliver as per those. The tech leads or project managers would also own the identification and mitigation of risks during the project.

In an agile team, however, the limits posed by rigid traditional roles on individuals do not exist. Team members are encouraged to ask questions about the requirements of the product owners to seek clarification as needed. The conversation is an essential C in the three C's of user stories (Card - Conversation - Confirmation).

During the sprint planning or backlog refinement, the team members need to be courageous to ask the right questions to the business stakeholders. Team members need to put forth their views with courage and not succumb to pressure from the managers, tech leads or product owners during estimation to commit stories for the sprint. The team members also need to bring up the problems or risks they see during the daily scrum or even earlier than that, raising the red flag as soon as possible. They need to ensure that they are doing the right thing.

Sometimes, the organisational culture may take the courage shown by the team members in the wrong way of insubordination. This may hinder the team members from demonstrating courage. Coaches, scrum masters and leaders have a role to play in such a scenario to make the team feel empowered and psychologically safe to say and do the right thing. Use of clean language, alignment on the outcomes and rallying as a team might be some of the techniques to use in such situations.

During the sprint, the team members should not compromise technical excellence and good design quality in a rush to complete the committed stories. The team is responsible for product quality and needs to do all the right things to ensure the same. Effective use of the 'Definition of Done' as well as embracing engineering practices with a focus on automation can help to flag out things, such as code quality issues, failing tests and so on. When the team pays attention to technical excellence, technical debt does not mount up, and the development becomes sustainable.

The other part of courage is the team being ready to work on tough problems to accept new challenges and complicated stories. The work then becomes motivating and drives the team with the purpose to achieve greater heights. Courage in the agile teams paves the way for transparency.

Stories from the trenches

Here is a story where the waterfall legacy and the presence of the supervisor prevented the team members from showing courage when needed.

This team had members who had worked in the waterfall methodology in all of their previous projects. They followed their project manager or tech lead's advice on various aspects including technical design decisions, estimations and problem-solving or even to the extent of whether to help each other or not. It was very natural for them not to question any decision openly, as it may mean as questioning the authority or showing disrespect. The team did not lack talent or skills to bring the right opinions or suggestions to the table, but they lacked courage.

It took us, agile coaches, a lot of time to change this behaviour. We started with a discussion of courage as a scrum value and its importance to make the product successful. We encouraged the team to include it in the team norms. However, that was only a start and did not change the behaviour immediately. Initially, we made it a point to allow the team members to use anonymous ways to express their views, such as retrospectives.

We used the planning poker technique during estimation sessions to allow everyone to give their opinion freely. We collected qualitative inputs about team health through anonymous surveys. We brought up the inputs received from the team members during the common discussion and encouraged them to speak up to support their viewpoint. We explored various facilitation techniques from 'Liberating Structures' like 1-2-4-All or pairing up or discussions in small groups to gather inputs from everyone.

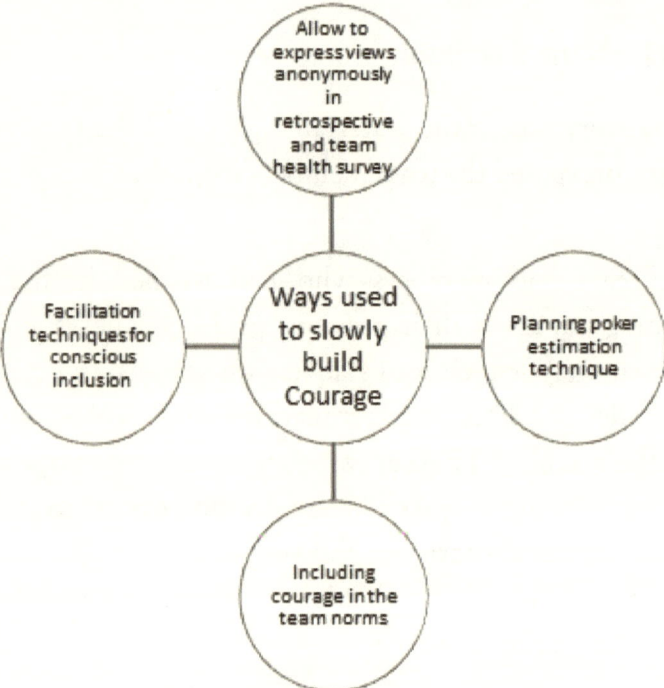

This gradually inculcated the habit of giving inputs and expressing their opinions to the team members, slowly building up their courage.

Read, Explore, Evolve

Encouraging team members to express their views every time could be the first step in bringing in courage. This means consciously practising inclusiveness.

Speaking in small safe groups help people to build courage.

Explore conducting the retrospectives in a variety of ways to encourage everyone's inputs.

Explore Liberating Structures that have several participative techniques, allowing everyone to give their inputs in coming up with options or decisions.

If office politics or culture come in the way of cultivating this habit in the team, taking help from an influential leader to handle the same may work.

FEEDBACK CULTURE

FEEDBACK CULTURE

"Feedback is the breakfast of champions."

– *Ken Blanchard*

Instilling feedback culture for both giving as well as receiving feedback goes hand in hand with the agile mindset to bring in transparency. It also helps agile teams to inspect, adapt and to improve continually. It is fair to say that agile methods work only when the teams assimilate the feedback culture.

Agile methods are people-centric, as we see in the first agile value of 'individuals and interactions over processes and tools.' When the interactions include feedback to make things better, it can lead to better self-organisation.

Agile teams imbibe the concept of empiricism and continuous improvement. Coaches and scrum masters should nudge and encourage teams to ensure that scrum events bring out feedback.

Daily scrum needs to be about feeding back on the progress. The team gives feedback about what is the appropriate set of stories that would fit into the sprint during the sprint planning. They also provide feedback about the stories of those who aren't in good shape to be taken up in the sprint. The sprint review is all about giving and receiving feedback on the product, and the retrospective is about the feedback on improving the ways of working.

The feedback about the product can also come from various technology enablers like intercepting points that provide the mechanics of frequently learning back about the system. Right from the code quality checking tools, automated tests and deployments to continuous integration keep feeding back information about the system.

ALWAYS LISTENING

The operations teams' continuous monitoring aspect gives feedback about the way the systems work in production, valuable feedback for the adoption of features in the business and the system performance for the development team. This feedback coming from both the development and operations teams about the product quality and performance helps the teams to make the product better.

Having a feedback culture to ensure that team members help each other grow by working on improvement areas is an excellent accelerator for the growth and development of the people. However, for that, people should feel comfortable in both giving feedback to others and receiving feedback from others. Psychological safety and trust are the two main pillars that ensure if the feedback can be given or taken.

Feedback culture from the perspective of people, process and technology, definitely helps the agile teams work the magic of agility and extend the path of transparency.

Stories from the trenches

Here are two stories about how the feedback culture helped two agile teams.

A team on its journey of the agile ways of working wanted to bring in continuous improvement and be better. Regular retrospectives brought in feedback on improving the ways of working and the regular sprint reviews brought in feedback on the product features. This helped them to be better as a team as well as build a better product. The team aimed at bringing the best out of its members, and hence resorted to building a feedback culture within the team, where people were encouraged to reach out for giving as well as receiving feedback.

This was a sensitive topic, as the people who gave the feedback or took the feedback may have felt uncomfortable. The team explored many different ways to accomplish this. First of all, the team established the ground rule of 'praise in public, criticise in private.' The team used an appreciative retrospective where they acknowledged the strengths of their team members and appreciated them. This helped in building a positive atmosphere within the team.

For constructive improvement feedback, the team employed a one-on-one approach. Individuals chose to seek feedback from others, as it is easier for a person to give feedback when someone asks for it. It sets the stage for listening to the feedback. The feedback provider, as well as the receiver here, treats the feedback to be a gift to make one better. This also helped in team building and creating an atmosphere of trust.

Here is another story on how the user feedback made a product more robust and better. This product was one of the most used products in the company but with a low user satisfaction score. The team decided to spend time in terms of seeking feedback from users on how the product was helping or not helping them through direct interviews and anonymous surveys.

After spending a sprint on collecting inputs from the end-users, the team and the business stakeholders were in for a surprise of the novel ideas they could think of to make the product better. The product has a much-improved user satisfaction score post-implementation of those ideas.

As a next step, the team also established mechanisms to learn from the adoption and usage in production through monitoring tools as a continuous feedback mechanism to improve the product.

Read, Explore, Evolve

There are several different ways of inculcating a feedback culture within a team. However, the team needs to have psychological safety and trust established. Otherwise, it may take the team members even farther away from each other.

People should receive feedback on how to be better in the future than as retrospective feedback.

Ensure that the feedback does not turn into a blame game session, and find out from the team about how the feedback sessions are helping them, course-correct as needed.

Collating, analysing and frequently working on user feedback are the critical aspects of making a product better. Explore automation in terms of capturing as much data about it as possible. However, user interviews and surveys remain as valuable ways to understand user sentiments.

MEASURE WHAT MATTERS

MEASURE WHAT MATTERS

"If you can't measure something, you can't understand it. If you cannot understand it, you cannot control it. If you can't control it, you can't improve it."

– *H. James Harrington*

One thing that helps teams in taking transparency to the next level and benefit from it is measuring what matters. Developing software without measuring the relevant data is like driving a car blindfolded. The various indicators on the car dashboard, such as the fuel left, the speed or the map with directions help us reach the right destination. Similarly, the right measurements help us get to the outcomes we want.

It is critical to measure whether the features rolled out in the software product are useful to the end-users or not. That helps the business stakeholders and the teams stay focused on what makes a positive impact on the lives of their end-users. This would also prevent them from simply being happy, pushing newer features to the users. The user adoption, value delivered, customer happiness score and the several other parameters available through the sophisticated analytics solutions, today feed the accurate data back to the business stakeholders, so that they can make the right decisions on the product's direction.

Measuring the right things help the teams to drive the teams' efforts most effectively by constantly improving their ways of working. The teams may benefit by measuring the team's productivity, capacity, speed, efficiency, effectiveness as well as product quality. When they measure certain things that matter and make those transparent, they would be able to bring in the improvement and become better.

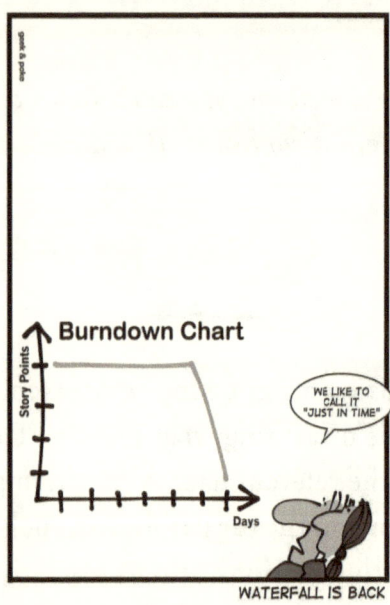

Measuring the right things can also bring the focus to achieving the outcomes rather than merely producing outputs. However, one must be aware of the potential problems that measurements can bring in, especially the standardisation of the metrics and mandates to achieve specific percentages that may drive different behaviours like compliance rather than continuous improvement or effectiveness.

Effective teams and stakeholders spend time to find out what value measuring certain things may bring to them, and then use those metrics to become better. That is probably the right agile mindset to inculcate.

Stories from the trenches

Measurements and metrics is a topic that is close to the heart of many. Stakeholders often demand measuring the progress and productivity of the agile teams to ensure return on investment.

One of the favourite metrics for managers to track is the velocity and burndown charts. However, it is well-established that people behave differently based on what is measured. People tend to change their ways of working for gaming the system. Velocity is an easy metric for teams to manipulate if needed, as it uses story points that are ultimately given by teams for the stories they work on. Managers should start thinking progressively on what they should measure to drive the right behaviour. Looking at various trends could be a good start, rather than focusing only on absolute numbers.

The measurements that the team agrees to understand their performance work the best. Conducting a session with the team to identify what matters to them to improve sprint on sprint gives a good picture in terms of possible metrics. Some of the metrics that have helped teams drive the right behaviour of frequent improvement are a say-do ratio, indicating committed work against the completed ones to denote the team's predictability, code quality metrics measured through tools, time to market, product quality metrics measured as production defects, mean time to recover, uptime and so on.

The other prime focus area is to measure and track the business outcomes. Here are some examples:

Business outcome example	Industry sector
On-time order fulfilment rate for orders	Retailer
Reduction of customers receiving incorrect bills	Utility company
Order lead time	Healthcare support product
Customer return rate	E-commerce organisation

Focusing on business outcomes can drive the team's behaviour in the right direction by eliminating waste, placing the focus on the right priorities and most importantly understanding the focus of why we are doing what we are doing.

Read, Explore, Evolve

I enjoyed reading the "Measure What Matters" book by John Doerr and can relate much to his suggestions on using objectives and key results (OKRs) as a way of life for organisations. Using OKRs has helped several teams I worked with in improving their focus and transparency.

A team coming together to define the metrics they wish to track is a win-win for the team and the management that wants to track the progress.

Sensitising the business stakeholders about identifying and tracking the business outcomes is essential to prioritise the right features.

PART 2

Ma	Make it transparent
G	**Genuinely collaborate**
I	Inspect and adapt
C	Continuously improve

COLLABORATION

COLLABORATION

"Talent wins games, but teamwork and intelligence win championships."
– Michael Jordan

Collaboration refers to the action of working with someone to produce or create something. The abstract and empirical nature of software development makes collaboration within the team and with stakeholders very critical.

Collaboration is different from co-operation, as co-operation is about helping or supporting each other while collaboration is about shared ownership. The collective ownership concept in scrum requires working together to serve a common purpose. The team offers commitment and is accountable for meeting the commitment.

The collaboration aligns the team with the business stakeholders to help them understand, validate, inspect and adapt. One of the crucial aspects of the agile manifesto principles states that "business people and developers must work daily throughout the project."

In the traditional lifecycle methods, the development team comprising of developers, testers, architects and such focus on completing the specific parts assigned to them. Individual ownership and accountability are restricted to the tasks assigned. The project manager is responsible for creating, assigning, integrating the appropriate tasks and for tracking those to closure. The business stakeholders give their requirements in a document at the beginning of the project and come back several months later to perform User Acceptance Testing before the production release.

The agile ways of working is a significant paradigm shift because of its collaborative nature. The business stakeholders need to work with the teams frequently. And, the team members need to work collaboratively to achieve their committed outcomes rather than only finishing their tasks.

This is not easy for new agile teams. It may prove to be challenging to move from an individual contributor to a collaborator's role. Team members need to listen to everyone and work together to figure out the best possible ways.

There are several examples for the lack of collaborator mindset. Team members may skip the daily standup meeting, as they see no value. They may provide a 'status update' of their stories before getting back to their work and disconnect from the discussion, and may also show disinterest in what others say. Some team members won't volunteer to help even after someone speaks of an impediment. They want to finish their own stories or help only if a manager suggests doing so.

Similarly, suppose the business stakeholders focus on pushing their requirements onto the team, without collaborating with the team to figure out the best possible way forward. In that case, they may end up not reaping the right outcomes.

Collaboration is at the heart of the agile way of working. Self-organisation, people centricity and customer-centricity can enhance the collaboration mindset.

Stories from the trenches

Here is a story of a team that went from an individual contributor to a collaborative mindset. The team worked on a product comprising of different technical parts.

The team was cross-functional, bringing all of the required technical skills needed. However, the team often failed to complete the stories in the given sprint. Some team members would complete their parts, but some others would not complete theirs, thus causing the story to spill over.

Even the stories reflected the type of work done by the team members such as 'back-end' stories and 'front-end' stories that would be dependent on each other. One would not be able to start working on his or her story until the other part has been completed. The daily stand up meetings reflected that some team members completed their parts while the others would be stuck due to the dependencies.

We conducted an experiment to finish a particular story covering all aspects of development, rather than breaking it into smaller pieces per individuals. Though the team was hesitant about this approach, they agreed to experiment. The team kept the story as a whole and did not break as per the technical parts.

Multiple team members came together to agree upon the interface or the skeletons to start with their parts. It led to meaningful conversations in the daily stand up. The team was able to see the progress of the story as a whole instead of having only pieces and complete the story within the sprint.

The team indeed learned the collaboration mindset through this experiment and went on to imbibe it.

Read, Explore, Evolve

Collaboration is an important aspect to make scrum teams successful. The scrum events of planning, review, retrospective or daily synchronisation will not be effective if the team does not collaborate.

Several different aspects, such as self-organisation, trust and consensus, are essential to bringing in the collaboration mindset in a scrum team.

It is also important to recognise the entire team for its achievements and not individuals.

The skills of working with business stakeholders as well as people need sharpening to bring about the collaboration mindset within teams.

SELF-ORGANISATION

SELF-ORGANISATION

"Hell yeah! Twitter was proof that leaderless self-organising systems could be true agents of change."

– Biz Stone, Things a Little Bird Told Me: Confessions of the Creative Mind.

One of the principles in agile manifesto states, 'the best architectures, requirements and designs emerge from self-organising teams.' For having the best of software crafted from our teams, it is vital to lead them to self-organising behaviour.

By definition, self-organisation, also called a spontaneous order, is a process where some form of overall order arises from local interactions between parts of an initially disordered system. The process is spontaneous, not needing control by any external agent.

Most of the examples in self-organisation come from nature, from forming of crystals to the movements of birds. Nature shows how local interactions in an initially disordered system can lead to a self-organised system. When someone hits a tree with several birds with a stone, the birds fly out in all directions without bumping into each other showing self-organising behaviour.

The self-organisation demonstrated by honeybees when they decide to form a new hive is a fantastic story. Bees individually travel to a certain distance in all directions from the existing hive to look for favourable conditions, come back, inform each other about their observations, discuss and reach a consensus by taking a decision among themselves based on the available information. Then all the bees that want to form a new hive fly to that location and start working on creating a new hive. Tiny insects can also figure out how to self-organise and benefit from that as a community.

The idea of self-organisation in an agile team means coming together as a team to think through the next best course of action to achieve the outcomes and be better than today. This eliminates the need for someone external to give orders or plan for the team.

The scrum events are all self-organisation events. Sprint planning helps to plan for a sprint, daily standup helps to plan for a day, reviews help to make the product better, and the retrospective helps to get better in the way of working. The team needs to take up these opportunities to self-organise.

Trust, psychological safety and scrum values such as commitment and respect go a long way to bring in self-organisation within the teams.

Stories from the trenches

I was talking to a team that had issues with its say-do ratio. Through discussions with the team members, it emerged as an issue with their self-organisation.

The developers in the team believed that the stories spill, as the testers are not able to complete testing. The testers expressed that the developers dumped stories on them for testing at the very last moment, not leaving much time for them to complete the testing.

We persuaded the team for a retrospective. The team thought of several ways to tackle this. The first way to tackle this was to slice the stories thinner. This will help the developers to finish it earlier. Secondly, the developers volunteered to help the testers to test the solution to speed up the testing process.

The third way discussed was to pair up the developers and testers early on to agree upon test cases to consider while developing or the last option was to add another tester to the team. By experimenting with these ideas, the team was able to solve their say-do ratio issue effectively.

The team needs to come together to solve their problems or decide the course of action to ensure that they progress well on their defined outcomes and commitments. That is what self-organisation is all about.

Read, Explore, Evolve

The self-organisation concept could be daunting for teams coming from a background where project managers controlled and directed the projects. However, one could always start small by inviting participation in decision-making. For example, in the sprint planning meeting, the coaches or scrum masters can invite people to pull stories and decide as a team of what they can accomplish in the sprint.

All scrum events are self-organising events. Discussing 'why' a particular scrum event and how to use it to self-organise can be a good starting point to imbibe the concept in the teams.

Leaders or managers play a vital role in the team's self-organising journey. They also need to take a learning journey to let go of control. They can ask the right questions or emphasise the importance of participation to make that happen. When leaders or managers take a step back and allow the team members' conversations to shape up the discussions and decisions, it is a step forward in self-organisation.

Engaging conversations, showing respect to each other's opinions and ensuring a psychologically safe environment could be an excellent starter to this cause.

PSYCHOLOGICAL SAFETY

PSYCHOLOGICAL SAFETY

"Safety isn't expensive, it is priceless."

Psychological safety refers to the safety people feel in their minds to express their opinions, concerns and feelings openly in the group. This is an essential ingredient for imbibing an agile mindset in teams.

Even teams with great bonding sometimes fail to raise red flags or speak up their minds, as they do not feel safe doing that. Team members hesitate to speak in front of their seniors or line managers, fearing that it might look inappropriate or negatively affect their career. Sometimes 'the customer is king' mindset stops people from disagreeing with stakeholders or in the context of a vendor-partner relationship. Other aspects, such as organisational hierarchical nature or command and control culture, may also play a role in creating an unsafe environment.

I often remember and quote the poem "The Charge of the Light Brigade" by Alfred, Lord Tennyson, where the soldiers were not to question the commands, though they knew it was a blunder and rode into a valley of death.

'Theirs not to make reply
Theirs not to reason why
Theirs but to do and die.'

With all due respect to the courage of the soldiers in this poem, today, in the complex problem-solving world, such as in software development, people need to show the courage to reason 'why' if they sense anything wrong in the decision made.

The team cannot create psychological safety for themselves. The ecosystem, such as the leadership or the stakeholders (line managers, HR, stakeholders, customer partners in a vendor partner scenario or even senior colleagues) plays an important role to create a safe environment for the team.

It is also critical for the team members to ensure that their peers feel safe to talk, discuss and express their opinions. Connections created beyond the actual work by spending fun time with each other, team building, talking beyond work, sharing and hearing about each other's vulnerabilities can help build up an environment of trust, and in turn, create a sense of safety within the team.

Great things can happen when all the skills and talent come together to solve the problems of today's Volatile, Uncertain, Complex and Ambiguous (VUCA) world in a psychologically safe environment.

Stories from the trenches

Leadership behaviour needs to change to bring in the required psychological safety in the teams. The leaders need to be willing to invest in it. Not all leaders may be ready for this, so it helps to identify the early adopters that are willing to experiment and change.

Here is a story about a group where leaders practised consciously to move away from command and control towards creating a participative and collaborative culture. First, they refrained from offering solutions right away. They asked people to express their opinion after discussing the problems. This showed the people that the leader cares about their opinions or thoughts.

The second was about being vulnerable. Everyone can make mistakes, but when the leaders are ready to accept their mistakes, it creates a humane connection. The third was about asking for critical feedback. In meetings or brainstorming sessions, a leader explicitly states that the team's opinion matters and welcomes a difference of opinion, as it brings up different perspectives.

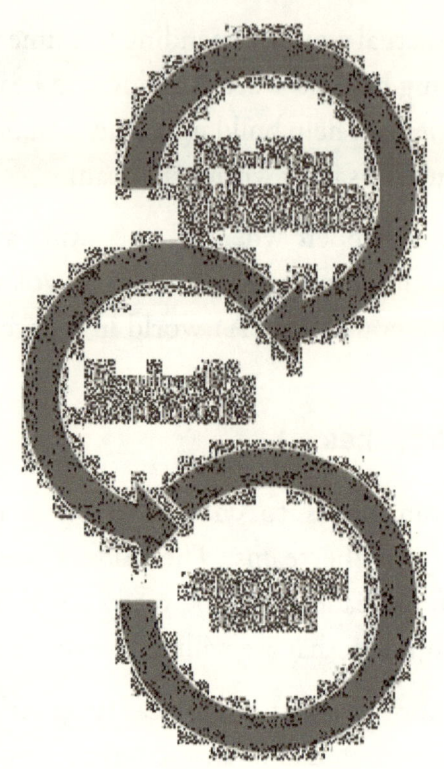

This made people feel safe, bringing up concerns or problems that they saw in what the leader had proposed.

Read, Explore, Evolve

I have often seen the concept of 'praise in public, criticise in private' working very well, where the team members can rest assured that the constructive feedback will be shared by the leader in private and not in public.

When the team sees that the leader acts on the team's suggestions, it visibly demonstrates that the team's opinion is essential and helps in taking the safety to the next level.

Events like hackathons and ideations inviting ideas from everyone to solve certain problems can fuel the team's willingness to speak up and contribute.

The team members feel safe when others consider an expression of disagreement with the majority's opinion positively.

The team needs to practice inclusivity and listen to different voices to come up with a common conclusion or consensus.

There is a cultural element to this aspect as well, where some cultures welcome dissent and some frown upon it. Recognising the prevailing culture where the team exists, the coach should plan a way to work through it.

External courses or discussions on leadership agility might help in instilling this thought process in leaders.

TRUST

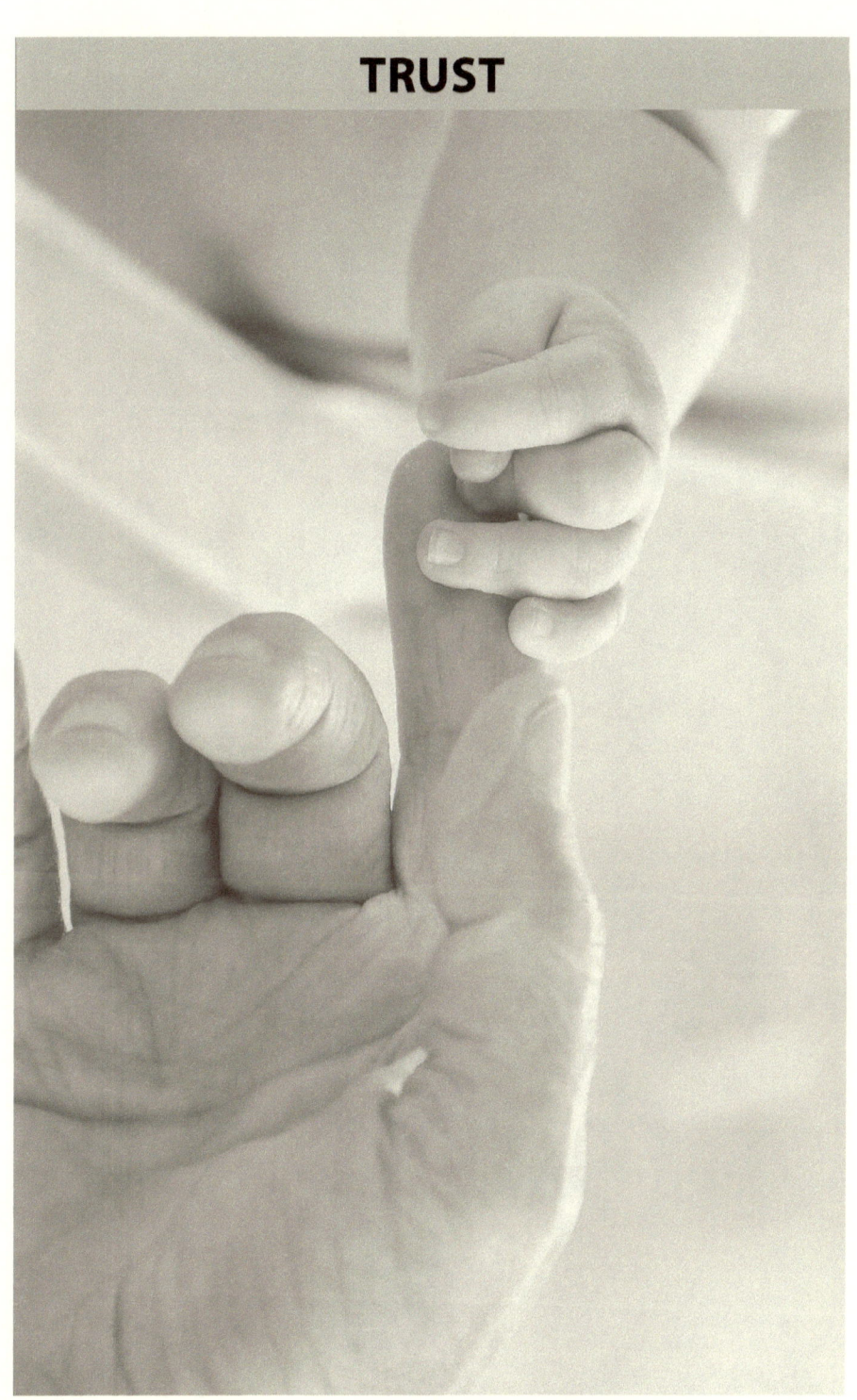

TRUST

"To be trusted is a greater compliment than to be loved."

– *George MacDonald*

The core values of scrum, courage, commitment, respect, focus and openness form the foundation of any successful agile team. To help the team imbibe the values of the scrum, the team needs the **right environment.**

The agile manifesto principle says, 'Give them the environment and support their need, and trust them to get the job done.'

When the leadership offers psychological safety to teams, it creates the right environment for the team. The team knows that they will receive support despite failures without blame or judgment. This helps them to learn, recover and become more effective.

There could also be a mistrust within the team itself. When the team members do not trust each other, it creates many issues in self-organisation and collective ownership. The mistrust may lead to **deteriorating the team's health,** resulting in several other issues such as longer meetings with no agreements and toxic conversations adversely **affecting self-organisation.**

There could be several barriers to building trust. One such barrier to trust could be the organisation structure. Team members may belong to different departments reporting to different leaders. The conflict among the leaders can transcend down to the team. Team members may feel that **proving their heroics** may give them a better chance in the career progression or other extreme scenarios. They may be working to safeguard their interests in case things go wrong.

This challenge needs a sensitive approach. As they say, '**most problems occur because people talk about each other but do not talk to each other.**' Honest and open conversations are the key to solving most of the issues within the team. **Face time** is another magical ingredient in the mix. When people travel across locations to meet each other periodically or engage in face-to-face conversations over a video conference, it helps to build trust.

Establishing common objectives and reiterating that the team wins or loses may help bring sanity in the conversations.

No cookie-cutter approach works when things are about people and their mindset. Every individual brings in an independent thought process, making the mix interesting and challenging. The interactions among the individuals set the right tone to solve these challenges.

Stories from the trenches

Here is a story of a team that had a lot of mistrust within itself.

The team members believed that every interaction was to happen over emails and documented. The team sent emails to each other (marking their managers in copy) if they needed any help. Blame-game was common in the case of issues where everyone tried to save their skin. Team members often escalated the team's internal problems to a manager or a scrum master instead of trying to solve it themselves.

It took a long time and over hundreds of conversations (both as a team and one-on-one) to change the toxic environment within the team. Here are a few things that worked for them.

Conducting a team-building workshop with games to bring the team together.

Exploring team outings, where team members could interact informally outside of the work setting. Team members could also share their interests and vulnerabilities.

Understanding the feedback game, where people shared their feedback with each other, treating it as a gift.

Open conversations were facilitated by a scrum master, coaching to set the team norms on how the team should handle conflict situations and work with each other.

Having face-to-face conversations rather than relying only on teleconferences helped. In-person meetings periodically were the norm for several teams that have geographically distributed team members. However, post-COVID, teams have embraced various video conferencing solutions such as Zoom, Google Meet, Microsoft Teams and so on.

One on one coaching for senior team members or leaders helped to enable an environment of trust within the team.

All of this was done taking baby steps, but the team enjoys a much better trust today working together towards better business outcomes.

Read, Explore, Evolve

Leaders can help bring an atmosphere of trust within the team by encouraging openness and transparency.

When the team sees that the leader does not single out individuals for failures, the safety created helps them to work with each other to get things done.

Encouraging team behaviour by rewards and recognition for the entire team through achievements would also contribute towards the team members trusting each other.

COLLECTIVE OWNERSHIP

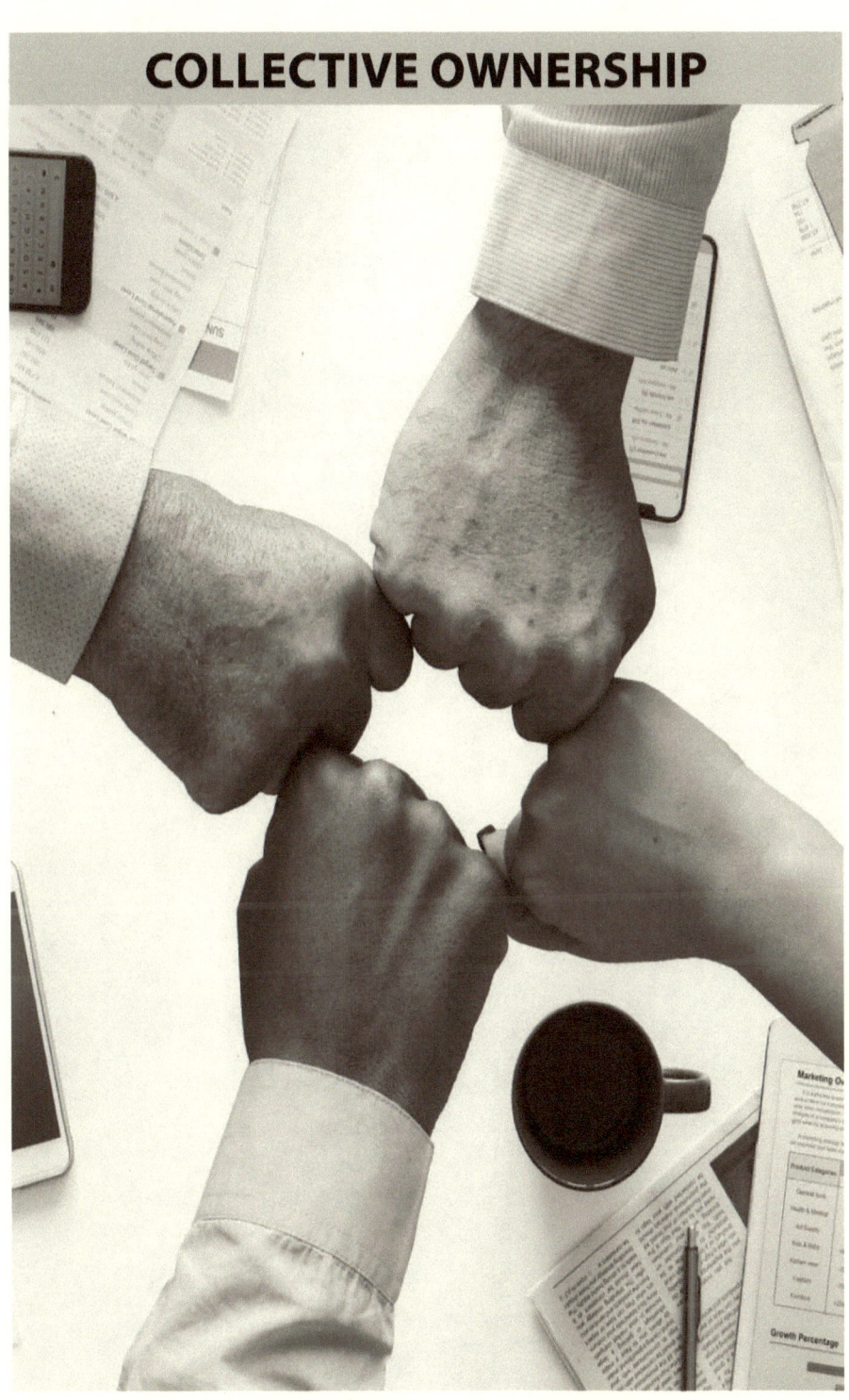

COLLECTIVE OWNERSHIP

"Effectively, change is almost impossible without industry-wide collaboration, cooperation and consensus."

– Simon Mainwaring

In an agile team, 'Collaboration' plays a significant role. A team collaborating and producing business outcomes matters more than individual contributions. Self-organising teams often come together to build consensus on topics of common interest.

Teams new to agile may be used to direction by others such as a project manager, a tech lead or a senior engineer. They now need to learn to build consensus among the team through discussions rather than following the instructions given by someone. They also need to learn consensus-building techniques. A consensus would often drive collective ownership, which is a critical element of self-organisation.

One example is the way the team estimates. Irrespective of whether the team uses relative or absolute estimation, story points, person-hours, t-shirt sizing or whatever, it is essential to estimate through consensus. When the team estimates through consensus, it creates a shared commitment and self-organisation.

The popular planning poker technique is a classic example of how the consensus-building technique can bring in diverse perspectives to the table. Build shared understanding and commitment within the team, rather than simply agreeing to the estimates given by one person, often a manager. I have used the video 'Agile Estimating and Planning: Planning Poker - Mike Cohn' to explain the technique to the team and pursue them to at least experiment with it. Despite initial apprehensions, teams usually see the value of the consensus-building concept during the experiment and embrace it.

The idea of having everyone put across their thoughts on a subject without getting influenced or biased by anyone, and then sharing their perspective can be liberating for people.

FIFTY SHADES OF RED

All scrum events, such as planning, daily scrum, reviews and retrospectives, need collective ownership. It is critical to ensure that everyone is comfortable bringing their perspectives to the discussion, be open to listening to the other's perspectives, and then build a consensus to take the decision. Every voice counts in today's VUCA

(Volatile, Uncertain, Complex and Ambiguous) world, as it is nearly impossible for one single person to come up with the exact solution and steps to achieve it.

There could be disagreements and different perspectives during problem-solving or deciding the future course of action. However, the consensus-building techniques can help in bringing it all together, to help the teams take collective decisions while agreeing to disagree. This goes in a long way to build a truly self-organising team that beams of trust and safety working towards customer delight.

Stories from the trenches

The shift from individual contribution to collective ownership is not an easy one. Here is a story of a team that was used to take up stories or tasks assigned to them by a tech lead, scrum master or product owner. Each member would estimate stories assigned to him or her. The other team members felt uncomfortable expressing their opinions on the estimation for someone else's story.

This meant that an individual would do the estimation, story and commitment for the sprint and not the team. If any of the stories remain incomplete, the responsibility of failing to meet the sprint commitment would be on that one individual and not the team. Team members often refrained from raising flags or for seeking help. They feared that the other members might question the estimation or commitment in such a case.

Discussions on the concept of collective ownership, encouraging team members to pair up for working on stories and starting tech discussions to cross-skill team members to learn various components of the system, slowly started changing this behaviour, thus leading to better outcomes.

Read, Explore, Evolve

Discuss the concept of collective ownership with the team, including the 'why' part of it. In today's VUCA world, multiple variables affect the outcomes and predictability. This demands multiple perspectives to solve a problem, rather than leaving it to a single person; however competent he or she may be.

Starting small by encouraging discussions within the group may be a good idea to begin this journey.

Proposing the idea along with inculcating the habit of cross-skilling within the team may also help iron out the skill or knowledge issues within the team. Maintain a cross-skilling matrix and a learning calendar to encourage sharing and cross-skilling.

Team events where everyone anonymously shares their input, such as in retrospective or planning poker could also be a good starting point to nudge the team for adding their inputs.

Another way could also be by creating a sprint goal during sprint planning, making people think about a common purpose that the team is trying to achieve during the sprint.

RESPECT

RESPECT

"Respect is a two-way street, if you want to get it, you've got to give it."
– R.G. Risch

Respect is one of the five values of the scrum. The scrum guide states that "Scrum Team members respect each other to be capable and independent people." The respect team members carry for each other becomes an essential ingredient in ensuring that the team matures towards becoming a self-organising team.

Respect for the capability and the independent way of thinking ensures bringing all perspectives to the table, something important to solve the complex problems.

One of the most sincere forms of respect is listening to what another one has to say. When scrum team members listen to the other person during their interactions, they show their respect. That paves a way to a collaborative culture over a command and control culture or one-way communication.

During the estimation of stories, the team members should respect each other's perspectives, opinions or risks raised, especially the senior team members can help the junior or new team members to speak up for demonstrating the respect for everyone's viewpoint.

HOW TO INSULT A DEVELOPER

During the daily stand up, team members should listen to what the other team members say to act on the early flags to help. Timeboxing also ensures that people respect each other's time and commitments. During the sprint retrospective, it is important to respect every team member's opinion, rather than questioning it.

Team members should feel empowered to point out any incidents where the individuals did not feel respected. This would help the team to be better by inspecting and adapting.

Openly asking for feedback, ensuring that each and everyone gets time to express their perspective in meetings, by going into discussions with questions rather than pre-conceived answers can be other ways in which one can pass on the message of 'everyone is respected.'

Respect for each other within a team paves the way for building trust and helps the team to reach a high performing stage in an accelerated fashion.

Stories from the trenches

I have often observed that if the organisation's culture and values talk about respect for individuals, it becomes easier to bring that to the teams.

I have worked with a team where a senior member often dominated the discussions and demeaned the opinions of the team members. Another team had an issue concerning a multi-vendor scenario, where the team member from the customer's side often overruled any points brought to the table by the vendor partner members.

These resulted in decreasing the morale of the team, prohibiting the team members from opening up and bringing their ideas to the table. This also led to weakening the performance in terms of missing commitments and a lack of continuous improvement.

The scrum master brought up this topic for discussion in the retrospective, along with the positive aspects of respect in conversations and its benefits. The team also decided to add it to the team norms to ensure that they all agree to the same and live by it. However, for the team members who often disrespected others, a one-on-one coaching session using powerful questions through the help of their supervisors to further aid in this coaching was necessary.

Read, Explore, Evolve

I love techniques like planning poker that help to ensure bringing in perspectives of individuals and encouraging discussions. These kinds of structures help in making it easy for people to speak up and listen by slowly building up respect.

Team members who show disrespect to others need different one-on-one coaching. Bringing in the intervention of supervisors to discuss expected behaviour helps.

As we interact more with people, we know them better and start appreciating their perspectives, developing respect in return. Allowing more opportunities for people to interact with each other to develop the rapport and respect would go a long way in creating an environment of trust and respect.

COMMITMENT

COMMITMENT

"Unless commitment is made, there are only promises and hopes… but no plans."

– Peter F. Drucker

Commitment in the traditional software development world typically refers to time or cost commitment for completing the given work. The famous iron triangle of cost-scope-time of project management suggests the project, cost and schedule would depend upon the estimation for the given scope. The term 'iron' here refers to all three of these remaining fixed once finalised.

Here's sharing some observations from my experience about commitments while using waterfall methods. A business reached out to the IT team with a business problem to solve. The IT solution team put together a solution design and a high-level rough estimate of the time and cost. The management would further reduce the 'ballpark' figure to come up with competitive pricing or bagging the deal.

Finally, some numbers in terms of cost and effort got 'committed' to the business, and the project landed into the lap of the IT delivery team. Now, the delivery team worked to honour the 'commitment' that 'they' never gave, often leading to burning the midnight oil or unpleasant discussions on who is at fault.

Agile methods reverse the iron triangle and encourage the scope to remain flexible while the time and cost remain fixed. The time remains fixed in terms of timeboxed iterations whereas the cost remains fixed in terms of the capacity of the team.

The commitment made by the team for the scope in an iteration is much more reliable and sustainable because it comes from the people who work on it. When the team closest to work being completed estimates the work for the next few weeks (not months or years), it is probably the best guess in the world than any analytics based on similar information or the kind of work.

The first value of agile manifesto states, 'Individuals and Interactions over Processes and Tools.' Rather than relying on certain estimation processes or tools that churn out a magic number of person-days, agile methods encourage relying on what the teams' best guess for a particular piece of work will be. The estimate is better, and the commitment is more reliable when the team estimates a small piece of work.

In a sprint planning meeting, team members decide the work they can commit to in the sprint. The team members use the 'Acceptance Criteria' and quality standards mentioned in the 'Definition of Done.' The scrum team based on an understanding of the requirements, skills within the team, the current state of the system, etc., formulates the sprint goal. As per the Scrum guide, "People personally commit to achieving the goals of the Scrum Team." The team commits to fulfilling the goal in the sprint.

SIMPLY EXPLAINED

The 'Ballpoint game' is one of the most popular games played in agile training sessions. It brings out many interesting observations. The team behaviour in terms of estimating, continuously improving and most importantly about committing as a team and living that commitment is a joy to witness. Wonderful things can happen when it does not matter who does what. In high performing teams, people jump to help each other to honour the team's commitment.

In today's world, where we do complex work, that needs more associate engagement, scrum's approach to commitment is probably the most relevant to bring out the best in people.

Stories from the trenches

Here is a story of a team from my early waterfall days. The team was in deep trouble, as they toiled to honour a commitment given by someone else. The team ate, worked, lived and slept (a little bit when they could) in the office to keep up with someone else's commitment. We used to joke about visiting 'sunshine.com' to get some vitamin D, as we would be in the office early morning until late evening.

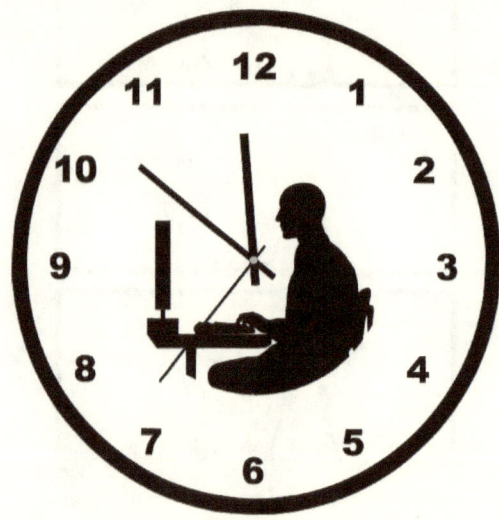

The situation was emotionally draining, and people often made mistakes under pressure. While the Human Resources team made efforts to boost up the morale, it never worked. This happened due to the fundamental issue of unreasonable expectations about living up to a commitment that was beyond what the team could fulfil.

The team had some brave soldiers who shone in need of the hour, and through their heroics, saved the battle to let the team win against the racing time. However, the sacrifices made by the team resulted in neither the team's happiness nor the business stakeholders.

I hope that this situation does not dawn upon any teams, and more and more organisations and teams embrace this 'commitment by people who do the work' concept. Teams take this commitment to the next level by measuring their predictability through say-do ratio that is measuring how much of the work they could complete against what they have committed.

Read, Explore, Evolve

One crucial aspect of commitment is that it needs to be a team commitment or shared ownership. If an individual gives the commitment and expects everyone to abide by it, there are dangers of falling through.

The team slowly discovers the capacity they have through the velocity trends of the sprints and can accordingly adjust their commitment in the sprint.

The culture of openness, trust and collective ownership helps the team to come up with a shared commitment during sprint planning.

When the team commits to achieving a certain goal within the sprint, the team can track it through the daily stand up meetings, raising early red flags.

The business stakeholders are also expected to commit to not bring in changes unless necessary to the team during the sprint. This would then help the team meet their commitment.

LIFE WITHOUT PROJECT MANAGERS

"The best way to find yourself is to lose yourself in the service of others."
– *Mahatma Gandhi*

Typical project management activities for a software project fall under conception, initiation, definition, planning, launch, execution, performance and project close stages. The project manager needs to perform these activities, create plans and track those to closure apart from identifying and closing the gaps between plan and execution.

When a team working in a traditional way of working switches to the agile ways of working, say scrum, they realise that the project manager is no more in their team. In scrum, several former project management activities become a part of the self-organising team's responsibilities.

The team identifies risks in various inspect and adapt events, estimates and plans each sprint. The team tracks the plan in daily standup meetings and continuously improves through retrospectives.

The team is empowered to figure out the most effective way of working that ensures quality and value. The team needs to give inputs in estimation meetings, ask clarifications to the product owner to understand the requirements, raise a red flag in the daily status meeting, pair up or help a fellow team member.

These are the new skills and new ways of self-managing the work. The team needs guidance on learning these skills. The new leader needs to prepare the team to take up these responsibilities and nudge the team to improve by inspecting and adapting in a psychologically safe environment.

Life without project managers for the teams is more demanding, but also more empowering and fulfilling.

Stories from the trenches

Here is a story of a group that had started a transformation to agile ways of working from the waterfall methodology. The existing project managers in this group were confused and not convinced about the new ways of working.

We had a good discussion with the project managers. They were, thankfully, open about their questions and concerns. They asked questions about how the typical project management activities happening in the agile world. They also wondered if things could work without project managers at all. It was a very fascinating and insightful discussion. However, the billion-dollar question was 'what next for them?'

It is natural to be anxious to see the role they practised for years does not exist anymore. In agile teams, managers no longer manage projects but enable people. The enablers ensure that team members get all the support they need—staffing and logistics support, solving impediments outside of the control of the team or doing performance appraisals as per the organisation norms.

Project managers from such groups often choose alternate career paths or move on to other groups that still have project manager requirements. While project management becomes a part of the self-organised team's working, the role of the project manager may not remain a significant role.

Read, Explore, Evolve

Here are the choices that project managers who choose to remain with the agile group can make. Some with interest in the domain or functional side get into a business analyst or product owner roles.

Some, who still have their technical skills sharpened, can join the teams to do development work, and contribute to the business outcomes.

Some with good people skills, and passionate about people development can get into the scrum master role. What will be required is to learn the responsibilities of the new role and competency required to succeed

This also, in turn, means that the team needs to pick up the aspects of project management.

EMPOWERMENT

EMPOWERMENT

"If you tell people where to go, but not how to get there, you'll be amazed by the results."

– General George S. Patton

Empowerment is a beautiful thing. One articulation of empowerment from a diversity and inclusion conference that struck the right chord with me was "Empowering someone means enabling them with all the support needed so that they can perform to the best of their abilities and potential with a motivation to be better."

Agile manifesto emphasises on 'Individuals and Interactions' leading towards self-organising behaviour. 'Empower teams' is also one of the seven principles of Lean.

In the context of agile teams, empowerment refers to the environment and support that the team needs to succeed. Leaders and managers help in bringing empowerment to the teams by changing the 'command and control' behaviour, supporting the team, and removing organisational impediments.

Rather than forcing one's opinions or decisions on teams, when the leader asks for the team members' perspective, it encourages the teams to speak up. Leaders of today need to bring in the servant leadership concepts. Servant leadership, initially coined by Robert

Greenleaf, is a paradigm where a servant leader takes care to serve other people's highest priority needs while leading them. A servant leader focuses primarily on the growth and well-being of people and the communities to which they belong. A servant leader surely brings empowerment to the team he or she serves.

Empowerment means that team members show courage in discussions, commit, fulfil the commitment and help each other to achieve the team's goals. They can bring the right questions to the table, to solve the problems and to help achieve the outcomes needed.

Team empowerment shows up when the team members participate wholeheartedly in the Scrum events, speak up to their potentials and contribute significantly towards the creation of value.

Stories from the trenches

I have worked with several teams that were genuinely empowered by their leaders who themselves were the agile practitioners and had seen the power of empowered teams.

They had embraced the concept of servant leadership. It is not an easy concept to digest, let aside imbibe and master. However, participative leadership reaps the benefits of collective wisdom.

Leaders demonstrating inclusive behaviour that makes everyone feel valued leads to empowerment

Read, Explore, Evolve

Team empowerment cannot happen overnight; it takes time and conscious efforts.

The first aspect is empowerment within the team, ensuring everyone feels empowered to contribute within the team. It is important to bring in the team bonding and for encouraging difficult discussions within the team. This helps to sail through the forming, norming and storming stages and accelerate towards the performing stage.

The second aspect is empowerment to contribute or question the status quo outside of the team. A leader who encourages the team to express their opinions freely and shows their own vulnerability to make mistakes empowers the team. Such a leader provides a safe environment for the team to succeed.

One important technique from the lean world for the leaders to embrace is Gemba or 'Go see.' This refers to leaders or managers visiting the place where the actual work happens to notice the real issues rather than relying simply on some status reports.

GEMBA

GEMBA

"Farming looks mighty easy when your plow is a pencil, and you're a thousand miles from the cornfield."

– *Dwight D. Eisenhower*

All right, I accept that Gemba is a lean concept and not from the agile manifesto or principles, but embracing this concept works wonders in the agile teams.

Genba (also Romanised as Gemba) is a Japanese term meaning "the actual place." Japanese detectives call the crime scene genba, and the Japanese TV reporters may refer to themselves as reporting from genba. In business, genba refers to the place where people create value.

In the manufacturing world, this concept is popular as a visit to the factory floor to identify process improvements. However, this concept appeals to teams as well as leaders as it encompasses getting to the value creation place. The 'Gemba Walk' or these visits help to figure out solutions to problems or spot new opportunities that may not have happened by sitting in air-conditioned offices looking at reports and guessing what would work.

Defining the right problem is the first step to solving it. Though several techniques help to define the right problem, nothing beats exploring the user experience by actually being with them. To see the issues faced by users the way they see it brings the needed empathy. The agile ways help to form a hypothesis and quickly churn out the solution to test it with the users, but the initial work of being to 'the actual place' helps formulate the right problem statement.

There is another way in which the Gemba concept can be useful for agile organisations. The concept of Gemba can be immensely helpful for leaders to come out of their corner cabins with a view to the place where the magic happens. No amount of surveys, feedback requests, open-door policies, audits or reviews can reveal the team's problems as the floor walks can.

Being with the team and talking to them at their workplace removes a lot of barriers and apprehensions from the teams' minds. Being a silent observer in scrum events can teach the leaders about potential problems or improvement opportunities against weekly status reports. Gemba is a wonderful technique for leaders moving into participatory leadership from a command and control one.

This simple yet very powerful concept of Gemba walks to understand that the team can help the leadership and understanding the end-users can help the business multi-fold.

Stories from the trenches

Here is a story from an agile team that worked on a highly used internal application in an organisation. Though the application had a million hits per day, the customer satisfaction score was relatively low at 3.8 out of 5. In its quest to improve the value delivered to the customer, the agile team thought about using the 'Gemba' concept.

The team identified a cross-section of users with diverse roles, experience levels and geographies, and met them to understand their point of view about the application. The team tried to understand how the application helps the users, how it is used, what is painful about using it and what improvements the users would like in the application.

The user interviews were very insightful for the team to understand the users' point of view. The team then worked with the product owner to think through the solutions, iterated the ideas with the users and implemented the same. Through this ongoing work, they achieved improvement in the customer satisfaction score, moving to 4.2 for the first time.

The 'Gemba' technique creates empathy about the users in the teams. A GE Healthcare case study presents a great example of understanding the user experience through Gemba to create a great experience for users. The team visited a healthcare facility for children where the MRI scans were a horrific experience for children. The team could empathise with their customers who were children through this Gemba visit. They redesigned the healthcare equipment using the 'adventure' theme to reduce the pain of the children coming for check-ups, bringing smiles to their faces. The case study is a must-see.

Read, Explore, Evolve

Empathise is the first step in design thinking where it is encouraged to connect with the users (preferably where they work) to learn from them about the problem.

Use the 'Gemba' technique to validate the hypothesis of the solution with users by being with them in their work environment.

From a leadership perspective, it is a new concept bringing in the people-centric approach. Instead of sending surveys or inviting people to come to the room to converse, simply observing without intruding or spending time with the team in their working place would be insightful.

CUSTOMER CENTRICITY

CUSTOMER CENTRICITY

"Happy customers are your biggest advocates and can become your most successful sales team."

– *Lisa Masiello*

The agile manifesto values 'customer collaboration over contract negotiations.' The agile manifesto principles also emphasise on making customer satisfaction as the highest priority and harnessing change for customer's competitive advantage. Customer-centricity is thus a critical part of an agile mindset.

The agile teams treat the product owners as the customer or representative of the customer. The product owner is the authority for content and priority. However, the product owners simply represent the end-users. The product owners learn about the wants and needs of the end-users through various means such as user research, market research, product usage analytics, pain points obtained from user feedback and so on. Product owners also ensure to use the voice of the customer to prioritise the product backlog. However, the product owner is still not the end-user or the customer.

Typically, the agile teams' interactions are restricted to the product owners. However, agile teams benefit when they interact with the stakeholders and the end-users. After a critical feature production rollout, the team interacts with the end-users to explain it to them, participates in roadshows, hence helping the product owner in the user adoption. The team enriches its knowledge about how the users use the systems. This Gemba walk helps them to make their contribution to the product more meaningful.

A customer-centric team seeks to understand how a requirement would help the end customer, it's 'so what' and the reasons for the priority assigned. This enriches the 'acceptance criteria' or 'confirmation' part of the user story through meaningful 'conversations.'

Customer centricity also drives the agile teams to build in the automated techniques to get feedback from the end-users, such as product usage analytics and monitoring tools.

SIMPLY EXPLAINED

MAXIMUM DIEABLE PRODUCT

The product owners with the customer-centric mindset step up their contribution by engaging in relevant user experience, design thinking and other user research methods. Customer-centricity helps them to build the right thing.

The lean startup concept of 'Build-Measure-Learn' also emphasises the benefits of measuring the user's response to the built system and learning from it. This is a great way to ensure that the product is customer-centric.

Bringing in customer-centricity as a thought in the team's minds is probably the biggest win for instilling the agile mindset.

Stories from the trenches

The customer needs to be at the centre of everything the agile teams do. An agile team wanted to improve their product's adoption. They sent out surveys to the customer groups post the product rollout. This helped them to understand the pain points of the customer, make the product better, eventually leading to better adoption. The team also put up several measures to track the adoption, and used it to validate the new features of the product.

Another agile team promised their business stakeholders to improve the number of processing records per day through their system. This led them to perform the value stream mapping to identify waste. The team brought in automation to reduce the identified waste and improved the record processing speed.

Customer centricity helped these teams to find their purpose, and make their work meaningful, rather than just churning out pieces of software each day.

Read, Explore, Evolve

Focus on business outcomes helps to nudge the teams to think about the right metrics to measure what matters to the end customer. It sows the seeds of customer centricity in teams.

Constantly questioning how a requirement would help the end customer is the key to get there. When any new features, stories or tasks come in the way, the team should attempt to understand how this makes the users' life easier.

The operations teams demonstrate customer-centricity by measuring the adoption, other user metrics or by analysing the root cause of incidents. They can feed it back to the development team or the business stakeholders.

The operations teams can also focus on improving user-centric metrics, such as uptime or mean time for recovery to ensure that the customer experience is better.

WORKING WITH BUSINESS

WORKING WITH BUSINESS

"Your most unhappy customers are your greatest source of learning."

– Bill Gates

Agile methods consider 'customer-centricity' as its core. A principle of the agile manifesto says, 'Business people and developers must work together daily throughout the project.' The interaction of business people with the development team is a key to ensure customer-centricity. It also gives a purpose to the team's work.

However, working with business people may not come easy to developers. The development team may prefer to work on their computers alone. They prefer someone, such as project managers or business analysts, to tell them what to do. The development team members may be uncomfortable talking to business people due to various challenges such as communication skills issues, lack of business domain awareness, not seeing the value in interaction with business and so on.

In reality, there are no IT projects, but only business projects or business transformation enabled by IT. IT projects exist for a business reason. If there is no business reason, there is no IT project. Teams need to understand this to start looking at interaction with business not as an interruption but as an opportunity to enable great business outcomes.

Interaction with business is an opportunity to co-create a product by giving valuable technical inputs to the business. Technical implementation is just an enabler to bring the ideas of business about the product to life. What better than to hear from the original thinkers themselves on what needs to be done? Sometimes requirements might be technically difficult, not feasible, or the sequencing may be inappropriate from an implementation perspective. The development team can flag it up. It is also an opportunity to trade off complex work for high-value work by providing alternate solutions.

AGILE FAMILIES

MAKE SURE YOUR USER STORY IS CORRECTLY PHRASED

Feedback from the business is the real feedback for the team's work (though the feedback of the end-users would be the icing on the cake). Why miss such an opportunity? The business and development team engaging in open and honest conversations is key to achieving great business outcomes.

Stories from the trenches

Many times I have dealt with the issue of reluctance from developers and testers for talking to business stakeholders periodically. They say, 'leave me alone to do my job.' There may be several other problems such as business communication, articulation or the issue of technical jargons.

The development team is too deep into the technical implementation and may use technical language while explaining impediments or issues. This may create barriers with business when they do not understand the technical language.

In most cases, it takes time and various means such as training on improving business communication skills or the art of articulation to build this bridge between the business team and the IT team. A discussion on why this interaction of the agile team with business stakeholders is important at various events.

Read, Explore, Evolve

If the agile team is not actively participating during interactions with businesses, such as sprint planning, reviews, backlog refinement or any other meetings, it is important to take up this point for discussion.

The skill issues are addressable through training, as several courses are available for the same.

Focus on simplification and bringing in the thought of how a particular point in discussion impacts business is very critical in smoothening the communication between the business and the IT team.

The typical bridge is the product owner; however, the product owner can help the team to step up and create an information highway across the business and IT.

As always, the golden rule would be 'praise in public, critical feedback in private.'

PART 3

Ma	Make it transparent
G	Genuinely collaborate
I	**Inspect and adapt**
C	Continuously improve

INSPECT AND ADAPT

INSPECT AND ADAPT

"We" are the empirical decision-makers who hold that uncertainty is our discipline, and that understanding how to act under conditions of incomplete information is the highest and most urgent human pursuit.

– Nassim Nicholas Taleb, The Black Swan: The Impact of the Highly Improbable.

'Inspect and adapt' is a foundational pillar of agile thinking. The idea of doing something (preferably working software in a short iteration), inspecting it, taking feedback and then adapting is a key to ensure that we traverse the right path and create the correct value.

I would like to draw your attention to a very popular leadership framework for decision making. The 'Cynefin framework' explains the theory behind Scrum. This framework divides situations or problems into five domains—simple, complicated, complex, chaos and disorder. It proposes different ways of decision-making to deal with it.

The obvious situation, the domain of 'known-known,' is the 'Simple' context where one can sense the situation, categorise and respond based on already known best practices, for example, typical business operations. The 'Complicated' context is the domain of known unknowns, where experts can sense, analyse and respond by bringing in their good practices, like the consulting domain.

The 'Complex' context is the domain of unknown unknowns where there are too many variables and interactions across those at play to predict the outcome of any process confidently. In such a case, the relation between the cause and effect can be known only in retrospect; practices are emergent. This is where the probing the problem statement, sense and responding in retrospect helps. As things are unknown, it is essential to retrospect to confirm the hypothesis and correct the course. The 'Chaotic' world is where the action needs to happen first.

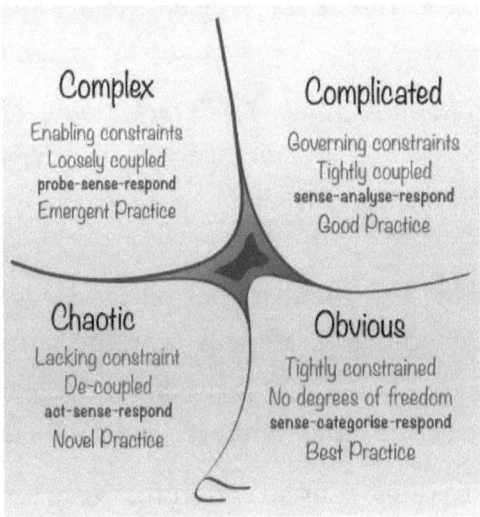

Source: Wikipedia

We need emergent practices to solve complex problems such as software development. The relationship between cause and effect can only be perceived in retrospect. Empiricism is a theory that believes that all knowledge stems from the experience derived from the senses. Using experiential learning to discover the next steps is a better way to draw up a future course of action in software development, than relying on only one person's guesses.

Coming up with working software based on what the users or stakeholders asked for. Showing it to them or letting them use it, and learning from the feedback is the key behind delivering real value to the customers or the end-users. This helps in churning out things that the users need versus what they thought they need or wanted.

This is where inspection and adaptation pillars of scrum shine. The abstract and empirical nature of software development makes a case for a **collaborative and iterative development approach**, the essence of agility.

While the empiricism brings benefits through iterative and incremental ways of working, several different concepts such as focus, simplicity or prioritisation, and techniques like time-boxing and cadence help bringing empiricism to life.

Stories from the trenches

I have done training programs for several teams who were used to waterfall methods with big upfront planning and a lot of documentation. The documents supported the various phases of requirements management, architecture, design, development, testing and release.

They had several questions on why they should care about the agile ways of working. They perceived the 'inspect and adapt' concept as a trial and error method. They believed requirement analysis needs time to detail exact business needs. They also believed in a phased approach to take the business needs to reality.

Among several discussions with the team, one interesting discussion was about how software development is different from a typical civil or manufacturing process in terms of having a waterfall setup. In a civil or manufacturing world, things are concrete, and the engineering practices are more evolved and standardised.

The blueprints and floor plans of the amazing structure are very important and are ready before laying the foundation. A lot of thinking about architecture and design needs to go in and documented in this field, down to a large amount of detail so that the engineers, supervisors and labourers on the ground know what exactly they need to do.

This influenced the initial thinking in the software world. The end-users explained their wants. Then the experts came up with their thinking and guidance down to the level of implementation to build the system. However, structural changes post-completion of the construction is not very common in the field of the civil or manufacturing world.

The software community always has to deal with changes once the software comes to life. While the business feels something was implicit, the IT team points out that it was not present in the requirements document signed off by the business resulting in the blame-game. There are also issues for the contracts and negotiations about that. I believe the abstract and empirical nature of software is responsible for this dilemma.

The abstract nature of software refers to the fact that the business or even end users may not know what would work for them until they try out options and use the developed system. Software being abstract, it isn't easy to imagine exactly how it would help. The various user research techniques and prototyping before actual development is a good way to smoothen the process, but those still cannot replace the experience of actually using the system.

Read, Explore, Evolve

'Inspection' part of the empiricism process for the product is seeking feedback from the product owners and business stakeholders during the sprint review.

'Inspection' for the way of working is to reflect in the daily sync up on the progress as well as the sprint retrospective.

'Adaptation' for the product happens in sprint planning during the prioritisation of the work for the next iteration. Through daily the stand-up and retrospective, the team identifies better ways to create value.

FOCUS - BEING PRESENT

FOCUS - BEING PRESENT

"Concentrate all your thoughts on the work at hand. The sun's rays do not burn until brought to a focus."

– *Alexander Graham Bell*

In today's 'Always On' world, it is very easy to get distracted. Notifications on our phones or laptops dictate what we focus on next. New emails with subjects like 'urgent' or 'last date' keep grabbing our attention away from work. Instant messages on collaboration tools such as the HCL Sametime, Slack, etc., are never-ending. The phone calls are even more intrusive.

We have become a multi-tasker and take pride in being so. In our personal and professional life, doing many things at a time seems to be the order of the day. Each one of us has multi-tasked at least once to attend to that important email from our boss while we were on another conference call. We were present at the conference call, but not fully present.

Multi-tasking has an immense overhead of task switching or context switching resulting in the loss of productivity and efficiency. Doing one thing at a time with full attention often yields better quality of whatever we do than doing two or more things at a time.

'Focus', one of the five Scrum values, refers to doing only a few things (maybe just one) at a time, doing it well, and taking it to closure. According to the scrum guide, "Everyone focuses on the work of the sprint and the goals of the scrum team." Though there are a hundred things on the backlog that need to be done."

Scrum tells us to pick up the most important things that can be done in a sprint duration and complete those in the sprint. The Scrum Master helps the team to maintain this focus by shielding them from the outside interference or engaging in any non-valuable things.

The user stories that individuals own or the tasks they create help them to focus on the work with the best possible quality without getting distracted.

SIMPLY EXPLAINED

People practise various techniques to improve focus. I have practised 'quiet time' blocked on my calendar to ensure I do not get disturbed at a particular time by other tasks. I have seen people using 'do not disturb' flags or hanging 'do not disturb' umbrellas at their desks to focus. 'Pomodoro' is another technique that helps one focus on a task for a pre-defined time, usually 25 minutes separated by short breaks. Some people log off at the same-time on slack or emails during their focus time of work.

"Stop starting, and start finishing" is a lean technique to keep focus, and ensure that only a few things are started and taken to the closure before new things start. Other techniques like time-boxing and cadence are extremely useful to keep the focus of teams.

I believe 'Focus' could be a good friend to have in today's all-distracting world. It can bring up the most important things worth our time and create value for whomsoever-it-concerns.

Stories from the trenches

Here are a couple of examples of how we get distracted often in our daily lives from whatever we are doing now.

Scene 1 – In a scenic Kerala Spice Garden, a family is taking a guided tour of plants, spices and medicines. One person gets a call on the phone and takes it, citing it is an important one. While he takes the call on the phone, he suggests the facilitator go ahead giving the information. The facilitator refuses and says, "I will wait, I want your full attention." I found the facilitator's take on waiting for focused attention from his customer impressive. He wanted to ensure he could get his points across, no multi-tasking, please.

Scene 2 - A couple sits down for having a morning cup of tea and breakfast together on the dining table. However, the overnight WhatsApp notifications and news apps are tempting them to get busy on their smartphones. They are present in front of each other, but not entirely present. They are lost in their virtual world, compromising the quality of their valuable family time.

Focusing on a few things, and getting those done is much better than doing too many things and achieving little. 'Stop starting and start finishing' is the key.

Many digitally native companies such as Google focus with OKRs, i.e. Objectives and Key Results, where Objectives indicate goals and Key results indicate the measures. It is helpful to have 3-5 objectives and 3-5 key results per objective to maintain the focus.

Read, Explore, Evolve

Sprint planning helps the team to choose from a prioritised list of stories, the first step towards a focus on the most important backlog items.

A sprint goal aligns with the focus of everyone on the team. The team can then self-organise their work to focus on achieving the sprint goal.

Daily stand up meetings also ensure that the focus on sprint goal and commitment is reiterated. The impediment that may come in the way of achieving the sprint goal ensures the focus.

Kanban teams focus on improving the flow and getting things from left to right as soon as possible to help improve the throughput.

TIMEBOXING

TIMEBOXING

"Nothing makes a person more productive than the last minute."

For all of the busy bees that we are, always occupied with something or the other, here is something to think. The Parkinson's Law states 'work expands to fill the time available for its completion.'

Every day we need to finish many daily chores, be it cooking, packing the lunch boxes, getting the kids ready for school, putting the house in order, getting ready for work and so on. Though those should take a similar time each day, it often ends up taking a different amount of time on different days depending upon the time we give it. Especially the chores like cleaning up rooms and tidying up things seem completely dependent on the time we allocate to it. Those tasks are time-consuming monsters; eating away whatever time we throw at them.

The same is the case with many things in our work environment, such as creating a PowerPoint deck for the presentation, authoring a white paper or a newsletter or even writing an important email. There always appears to be a better way of doing it.

Timeboxing simply means 'Put a time box around your tasks' or allocating a maximum time for a task. It is amazing to see the results of this technique at the office as well as at home. When we allocate finite time to complete something, we automatically prioritise and focus on the most important items.

Scrum considers timeboxing very important for its events. The timeboxing of the sprint to up to four weeks ensures the team focuses on the most important things for the next one to four weeks. This gives the much-needed predictability to the business on when they can expect at least some of the high priority requirements to be completed.

Timeboxing of the scrum events (or meetings) is a boon to everyone, ensuring that the team focuses on fulfilling the sprint goal.

Stories from the trenches

The concept of timeboxing is a boon to many teams that suffer from endless meetings syndrome. A team that I coached suffered from this issue of daily long problem-solving meetings with discussions not relevant to everyone. No one raised any objections as some senior stakeholders and managers were involved. The senior stakeholders wanted to know the updates from everyone, hence resulting in micro-management.

Finally, one of the team members showed the courage to bring this up in the retrospective. The scrum master suggested strict time boxing. Timeboxing proved to be a wonderful remedy to this issue of endless meetings. Post-usage of the timeboxing technique, everyone became conscious of the time and started prioritising the discussion topics. The team members reminded each other of the time left and identified things to be discussed offline with only a subset of the team.

A team claimed that they are never able to complete their daily stand up in 15 minutes, as there is so much to discuss. We explored various options to use the daily stand up only for team synchronisation, bringing up impediments, and ensuring the problem-solving happens in a meet-after. This helped the team members who would often feel disengaged in the meeting as the discussions were dragged.

Read, Explore, Evolve

We should never compromise the timeboxing of iterations or sprints. Teams should not fall into the trap of increasing the sprint size by a day or two to complete a few pending tasks. Following fixed-length iterations brings a lot of discipline, cadence and focus on the way of working for the teams. If the teams are consistently failing to deliver any value in sprints, the teams can revisit the duration; however, should still time box it.

Timeboxing meetings drive the discipline and predictability in the way of working for the team. Whether planning, review or retrospective, timeboxing allows the teams to focus on outcomes, and get the right value out of the time everyone's spending together.

Timeboxing in every interaction or meeting (be it design discussions or problem-solving) also ensures focus and outcome-orientation.

Finalising agenda in advance, preparing well for the meeting, circulating the agenda in advance and setting the expectations of participants helps to get value out of meetings and timeboxing.

CADENCE

CADENCE

"Harmony is the inner cadence of contentment we feel when the melody of life is in tune."

– Sarah Ban Breathnach

Cadence refers to a **rhythm** or a **heartbeat** of the team. Cadence is a great way to transition to **predictable events** than running behind the so-called 'deadlines.' Scrum has some great advice in terms of events based on cadence to bring predictability. These events make the interactions between the team and the business stakeholders to plan and review progress predictably. These also help team members to come together to synchronise their work daily.

"Cadence and synchronisation limit the accumulation of variance" as Don Reinersten, the author of 'Principles of Product development flow,' states. According to SAFe™, cadence applied to teams turns unpredictable events into predictable ones, thereby reducing costs and making wait time for new work predictable. When the business has a new idea to bring to the development team, they can bring it up in the next sprint planning meeting and prioritise it over other items.

LEARNING AGILE

Teams must continue to work on a cadence with respect to scrum events. Sometimes teams question the need for a daily stand up given that they are co-located and talk all the time during the day with each other. However, the daily scrum meeting still establishes a formal platform for everyone to synchronise. Sometimes teams working together for a longer time feel that retrospectives are repetitive and boring. However, the cadence for retrospective meetings helps in bringing in focus on continuous improvement to the teams.

I believe that if there is no cadence set for something that is supposed to happen multiple times, the chances that those discussions do not happen are quite high. This is true even with mentorship, learning discussions and our personal goals. **Combine time boxing with cadence, and you get a great recipe for successful execution to bring focus to work.**

Stories from the trenches

I have seen great examples of maintaining a cadence of activities, meetings or reviews, always helping teams achieve better outcomes.

Communities of practice within an organisation survived for years and thrived when they committed to a cadence to learn and share. The cadence helped them to self-organise, and be prepared to fulfil their purpose.

In another organisation, the quarterly cadence of setting OKRs (Objectives and Key Results) and monthly check-in cadence helped teams to stay focused on what is most important as well as tracking that to closure.

I have also reaped benefits of setting up cadence for discussion with my mentees as well as my mentor so that there is a fixed time booked for discussion helping in continuous feedback.

Read, Explore, Evolve

Treat the sprint cadence as sacrosanct, do not accept to change it or accommodate any extensions.

Ensure that the teams follow the cadence of sprint planning, daily standup meetings, sprint reviews and retrospectives. If there is a hesitation in following the cadence, work with them to ensure they understand 'why' behind each of those events.

Especially for retrospectives, observing cadence is very important only next to ensuring effectiveness. A coach had once mentioned that retrospectives are like brushing our teeth, we can skip it, but then we know what happens when we skip it. To ensure that we constantly understand the waste and issues, we must remove those to run effective retrospectives on cadence.

'Develop on cadence, release on-demand' is an amazing phrase made popular by SAFe™. When we develop the business requirements and churn out working software on cadence, it gives the business the desired predictability.

SIMPLICITY

SIMPLICITY

"Simplicity is the ultimate sophistication."

— *Leonardo da Vinci*

While discussing the agile manifesto principles with teams that are new to the agile ways of working, they often get confused with the simplicity principle. '**Simplicity**—the art of maximizing the amount of work not done—is essential.' While the word 'simplicity' is pretty clear and obvious to people, the part '**the art of maximizing the amount of work not done**' confuses people. I too have faced questions from people asking whether it is 'maximizing the amount of work not done' or 'maximizing the amount of work done.'

Here is an attempt to understand a simple but very powerful principle. Lean, Extreme Programming (XP) and scrum practices or techniques demonstrate this principle often.

In XP, one of the rules states that one should 'Do the simplest thing that could work next.' The idea is to focus on keeping the design or implementation of the code simple. Any complex work often turns out to be expensive, as it becomes difficult to understand, maintain and refactor. Once the team understands the requirements, they can think of the simplest thing that could implement the given requirement or solve the given problem.

The practices like **'Test-Driven Development'** further drive this behaviour by first writing a test case for a given requirement, and then thinking about the simplest solution to pass the test. It is possible to come up with a simple design and code for even complex problems if we try to break it into smaller chunks and attack them one by one.

Lean philosophy drives the idea of **'eliminating waste.'** Waste refers to the unnecessary work done in the process of producing value. It is very important to ensure that we identify and eliminate waste or unnecessary work.

In agile ways of working, the **focus is on the value and outcomes**. Keeping things simple and prioritising the most valued items often drives that focus. Ensuring that the product backlog is always prioritised based on value, maintaining to strip it off any unnecessary items would ensure that we maximise not doing things.

The 80-20 principle about features that states that 'Only about 20% features are used by 80% users' also supports the simplicity principle. The rest of the 80% features thought with a lot of care by product managers and implemented with a lot of love by teams remain mostly unused. All the scrum events amplify this principle as the team focuses on backlog items and goals committed for a sprint.

However, ensuring simple design or code, eliminating wasteful work, prioritising the most valuable work are not easy practices to master. It is an art where one develops mastery through thoughtful practice.

This is how the 'simplicity' principle ensures the focus is on producing value, keeping things simple and maximising the amount of (not so important) work not done.

Stories from the trenches

I've been using an Apple smartphone for many years, and one of the many things I admire about Apple products is the simplicity. Focus on the user has probably helped the designers and developers to keep things simple.

No one wants clutter in the products they use. The user experience is better when the product is simpler. As studies have demonstrated, people are not waiting for the next feature in the product, but they are looking forward to how the product makes their work simpler and easier.

Using the simplicity principle helps product managers to come up with a minimum viable product or a set of minimum viable features for the product. To make the products more desirable, it is important to keep those simple, de-cluttering, not adding features for the sake of it and always validating feedback before adding further complexity.

Several initiatives that I have driven have also benefitted from this focus on simplicity. Let me share a story about how we went about starting a company-wide agile conference. We kept it very simple as a teleconference with screen-sharing in the first edition. As people liked the idea and expressed a desire for a face-to-face meeting, we used video conferencing across locations in the next edition.

This helped us identify enthusiastic people across locations and organise the next edition as local chapters conducted in several locations as a physical conference. Keeping things simple and slowly building up things that matter to the users helped there.

Read, Explore, Evolve

Though we have spoken more on simplicity for the requirements, this is a principle that can help everyone to improve their outcomes.

Simple design, architecture and code make the products maintainable. Simplification should not be a separate initiative but built in the way we work.

Engineering practices such as test-driven development, refactoring, identifying and reducing technical debt, take us a long way into simplifying the software developed.

PRIORITISATION

PRIORITISATION

"Things that matter most must never be at the mercy of things that matter least."

– Johann Wolfgang von Goethe

Prioritisation is an essential ingredient for bringing in the focus on the most important things. Agile teams bring focus on value by prioritising work during the sprint planning. However, prioritisation is not an easy thing to digest for many business stakeholders. They believe calling out some features as less important than others may lead to not getting funding for those. That pushes the business to call out everything as an important and high priority.

Pushing everything as important instead of prioritising has many ill effects. Some of the ill effects are delay in feedback from the end-users, lack of a sense of achievement for the teams and the requirement deterioration.

'Perfect is the enemy of good' may prove to be the right discussion in such a scenario. Many times the idea of pursuing the 'perfect product' makes us lose outputting a 'good product' in the hands of the users.

I believe that the software requirements stated by business stakeholders or even the end users are nothing but a hypothesis of perceived benefits. End users either prove or refute it when they use the system. This makes it essential to use the MVP (Minimum Viable Product) concept to prioritise the product and features. That also helps to ensure that inventory of completed but not delivered work does not accumulate.

Product usage analytics often prove that a certain percentage of features of even successful products are rarely or never used, rendering the investment in building those fruitless. An approach of validating adoption and usage before investing further in the product is a smarter way to reap better returns on investment.

That is where it is very critical to emphasise the importance of prioritisation upon the product owners or business stakeholders who are reluctant to put a ranking on the requirements that they would want to go for implementation. Prioritisation techniques such as MoSCoW, Hundred dollars, Kano model and so on help the product owners to maximise value.

Conversations to prioritise, prioritise and prioritise will instil the behaviour change leading to simplicity in our products.

Stories from the trenches

A team was developing a product that was supposed to revolutionise a particular business process. I had a sneak peek into what was coming and was excited to use it. However, even after waiting for a couple of years, nothing came my way. When I enquired with the product team about the delay of the product release, the answer unravelled something I call the 'Big Bang Syndrome.'

The sponsors wanted to roll out a revolutionary product that would be a game-changer and kept adding functionalities to make it a 'game-changer' without taking it to the users or the market.

Though the example above is for a new product with a changed business process, this behaviour is common even for products or systems that replace the old ones. The urge to put all functionality available in old systems is omnipresent in migration projects.

We can address this 'Big Bang Syndrome' by coaching the sponsors on prioritisation as well as test and learn.

Read, Explore, Evolve

Thinking about prioritisation all the time helps to focus on the right things, as the time that we spend on important things is always limited.

Even in our daily life, focusing on urgent and important aspects maximises the value for ourselves.

It is helpful to have the product backlog in an always prioritised state, but if not always, at least during the sprint planning meeting, the prioritisation has to be present.

If the business wants to introduce any additional items within a sprint, the prioritisation discussion needs to happen. If something comes into the scope of the sprint, something else should go out.

PART 4

Ma	**Make it transparent**
G	Genuinely collaborate
I	Inspect and adapt
C	**Continuously improve**

CONTINUOUS IMPROVEMENT

CONTINUOUS IMPROVEMENT

"It doesn't matter how good you are today; if you're not better next month, you're no longer the agile."

– Mike Cohn

A self-organising and empowered team is trusted to get the job done without project managers. Many new teams and leaders wonder how such a team becomes high performing and what drives them towards efficiency and effectiveness.

To be better as a team, the team needs to imbibe a continuous improvement mindset that has a deep correlation with motivation. **What motivates people** is an area of vast research in the world of psychology. Several theories dig into that motivation aspect of the human mind.

One of my favourite theories in this context is the Daniel pinks book 'Drive' and the very well celebrated animation video on 'surprising truth behind what motivates us.' It proposes that **autonomy, mastery and purpose** are the three main motivators for people to do anything willingly. I agree with this theory wholeheartedly and believe that agile methods enable autonomy, mastery and purpose.

The teams are empowered to be self-organising. The scrum master shields the team from the outside influence. They aspire for mastery as they treat their work as a craft. Interaction with the business stakeholders to know what (and why) they need to do, getting feedback about their work gives them a purpose. This is where the motivation to do work increases as the team embraces the agile ways of working.

As the agile teams use **'inspect and adapt'** techniques like a **retrospective** to look back for improving their ways of working as a team, continuous improvement tickles in. As a first right step, the team identifies action items in retrospective meetings, discusses, agrees upon a few and prioritises. When the teams take up the improvement backlog item (at least one) as part of the next sprint and implement it, they move in the right direction of continuous improvement path.

Coaches and enablers can play an important role in making continuous improvement a habit in the agile teams.

To summarise, it is critical to take the teams on the continuous improvement journey by handholding them initially, and nudging them later to sustain the motivation, healthy and happy team environment and moving from being **good to great.**

Stories from the trenches

Agile teams embrace continuous improvement practice to be better every time. The teams use various retrospective techniques to ensure that they are on their path to be better. Many teams keep track of the action items brought up in retrospectives and make those visible to track it to closure. Teams that I have worked with have brought in improvement in terms of automation, fun events and knowledge sharing sessions to cross-skill, feedback sessions and innovative suggestions to the product and such through their retrospectives.

I also want to share a story of a team that was working together for a long time on the same product. They had a stagnation and started thinking that they no longer need formal retrospective meetings, as they are already very mature. We did an exercise with that team to draw up a timeline and mark **what they have improved month on month. This** proved to be a great mirror for the team to see for themselves that they need to step up their continuous improvement journey.

New or old, the same product or different products, short term or long terms, teams should not steer away from the path of continuous improvement if they want to bring agility to their work.

Read, Explore, Evolve

Retrospectives present a formal opportunity for continuous improvement to the team. Treating those as sacred and bringing effectiveness would help the teams to thrive.

The team must discuss the action items from the retrospective points, prioritise, own and put onto the backlog with visible progress made sprint on sprint. This ensures that the team trusts in this mechanism to be better and improves continuously.

Continuous improvement can solve a problem or enable opportunities. Bringing in the changing business and technology perspectives up for discussion may trigger thoughts on what next, what could be better and so on.

Ideathons, brainstorming sessions or *hackathons* involving the teams have paved the way for further improvement in the way of working for the development teams as well as the end-users.

Encouraging teams to share their learnings through sessions such as 'lunch and learn' or 'lean coffee' ensures the flame of continuous improvement is kept burning.

Celebrating wins even for a small thing that has improved something, motivates people to improve further.

Asking the right questions to the team regarding how they can be better if the team gets into a happy comfort zone.

Helping the team to see what good (or great) could look like for them. Any visioning exercise that compels the team to imagine where they wish to be in the future will help the team identify improvement areas.

Learning from other teams from the organisation or industry who have been continuously improving could be inspiring. Sometimes going back to the basics in retrospectives such as scrum values or the agile principles can trigger interesting conversations engaging teams to be better.

Making things visual (especially the progress in terms of improvements) helps exceptionally well. Sometimes there are systemic impediments in the path of the teams that prohibit them from being better. The enablers and leaders will need to help to clear those from the team's path.

EXCELLENCE

EXCELLENCE

"The will to win, the desire to succeed, the urge to reach your full potential, these are the keys that will unlock the door to personal excellence."

— Confucius

An important aspect of continuous improvement is instilling a culture of technical excellence.

In the traditional approach of software development in the 'Plan–Do–Check–Act' (PDCA) process, assuring quality is assigned responsibility for someone. A tech lead or team lead does the code review and points out issues. Functional testers detect functional defects in the code written by the developers.

In the agile methods, the team is responsible for ensuring the quality of the working software sprint on sprint. This calls for built-in quality. Quality is no more an afterthought or as being assured by someone else.

'Continuous attention to technical excellence enhances design quality' says a principle of the agile manifesto. Extreme programming (XP) philosophy advocates good engineering practices such as test-driven development, continuous integration and refactoring. Agile teams embrace these XP practices to the extent possible to bring the technical agility.

Technical agility and the pursuit of excellence in software development also bring up the topic of Software Craftsmanship (or crafts-person-ship). The coaches and enablers should treat software as a craft and encourage the teams to be pragmatic programmers. A software craftsperson is a responsible professional for the craft (working software) developed as any other good professional like a doctor, or a teacher would be.

Software craftsmanship manifesto takes the agile manifesto to the next level by raising the bar of professional software development by practising and helping others to learn the craft. It emphasises working on well-crafted software, steadily adding value while responding to change, developing a community of professionals while valuing individuals and interactions and ensuring productive partnership rather than just a collaboration.

Software crafts-person-ship philosophy coupled with engineering practices helps the team build quality in, and ensure sustainable development. This is an important link in bringing in the agile mindset within the team.

Stories from the trenches

I have been involved in instilling software crafts-person-ship and a good engineering mindset in several teams. I have heard several reasons why the team was not able to follow good engineering practices. It involves pushy sponsors, tight deadlines, business not willing to pay for automation to the simple reluctance of stating 'we have always done it this way,' 'it does not work in my technology' or 'we will do it once the system is a bit stable.'

To tackle one or more of these challenges teams face, and the perceptions they have, one needs to nudge the team about it constantly. Starting a discussion with the team about good engineering practices could be the first step. The enablement to the team needs to be by explaining why what and how regarding the engineering practices.

A step by step approach is often helpful, like first looking at automating code quality checks, unit test automation and then moving on to a higher prize like continuous integration towards frequent delivery. It prepares the team for the change mentally and makes the change rewarding as we achieve and celebrate the small wins.

Read, Explore, Evolve

The teams may take the time or resist adopting the practices due to various reasons. It would be important to understand the reasons, maybe employing lean techniques such as 5-whys to get to the root cause.

If it is a skill gap, suggest courses to take up, take the help of experts to teach and propose hands-on events like *hackathons* to experiment. Prepare a learning path that excites the team to progress on their learning in the engineering practices.

If it is a pushback from sponsors, talk to the sponsors on the importance of built-in quality. I have often seen sharing data for the time taken in testing or recurring defects. The time is taken for fixing defects helps ease this dialogue to focus on the outcomes from it.

Take help from senior leadership if needed, sometimes a message from the leadership helps faster alignment.

If it is a technology challenge to adopt engineering practices, it will excite the team to try out new things to make them better, hackathons with new tools could be helpful.

SUSTAINABLE DEVELOPMENT

"Sustainable development is a development that meets the needs of the present without compromising the ability of future generations to meet their own needs."

– Gro Harlem Brundtland

The shift from a classic project mindset to an agile mindset is an interesting change for teams. By definition, the project has a start date and end date, thus giving a structure to the work teams to do. The majority of the agile teams go on a sprinting release after release and delivering it to users.

The agile principle states that "The agile processes promote sustainable development. The sponsors, developers and users must be able to maintain a constant pace indefinitely." However, maintaining a constant pace through sustainable development may not be easy. I have observed a few challenges concerning sustainable development in the agile teams broadly in two categories.

For teams new to the agile, sustaining creation of working software, every sprint in itself could be a challenge. They might feel pressured or stressed. The idea of delivering working software, every sprint is scary for many new teams who are used to longer development cycles. Sometimes the teams start with a lot of excitement but struggle to keep pace or find that they have stories spilt over leading to unsustainable development.

Teams may be used to directions on the required work or delivery timelines, and hence tend to take up work that the business expects them to complete. They may or may not be able to complete it, trying their best or slogging it out. This may work in the short term, but it is not sustainable, and hence affects the team adversely.

Apart from empowerment and psychological safety, the team needs coaching on recognising what they may or may not be able to achieve in the sprint and talk about it openly to the business stakeholders. Using retrospectives to learn from the say-do ratio, challenging the team to improve the ratio or analysing why it shows up poorly, would help the teams to make their work sustainable.

One important enabler for ensuring the sprint on the sprint delivery being sustainable is the strong engineering foundation, such as automation in software development life cycle processes—

code quality checks, testing, integration and deployments. These engineering practices provide the necessary framework for sustainable development.

The other challenge I have heard is from teams that have been using the agile ways of working for long and know the practices or behaviours pretty well. These teams find the grind of delivering sprint after sprint meaningless irrespective of producing great outcomes for products.

The pursuit of excellence in software development or finding the purpose of the team could be helpful. Future-looking retrospective techniques like sailboat or letter from future apart from the periodic mission defining exercise for teams helping to address this. The teams themselves would see their higher purpose or improvement goals, and carve out their path to make their work sustainable and fulfilling emotionally.

Stories from the trenches

It is a key aspect to keep the development pace sustainable and ensuring that everyone involved understands this.

Once a team was completely frustrated and stressed out because of the 'new agile practices.' I figured out that the business stakeholders had interpreted the definition of agility to their advantage. They were asking the development team to incorporate required changes within the sprint, as the development team needed to 'respond to the change' as per the agile manifesto. They were not ready to negotiate on the stories committed during the sprint planning.

This caused issues for work the team had to put in and stretch themselves for customer satisfaction! Agile methods offer the flexibility to make changes to the requirements to respond to market needs and changing user demands. However, we need to couple this with the stability brought in by the timeboxing of the sprints. This will strike a balance between the chaos and complete rigidity.

Several discussions with the business stakeholders to explain the balance brought by the sprint cadence finally helped. The business stakeholders agreed that they would not disturb the team during their sprint by changing requirements unless it was super urgent. They also agreed to negotiate the existing scope in case of any scope changes within the sprint.

I have also seen cases where there is pressure on teams to maintain a certain velocity or teams that are questioned daily on how much work have they completed out of what they had committed by their business stakeholders or managers. This also creates unnecessary stress and makes the team feel like they are running on non-sustainable and never-ending sprints.

Coaches and enablers need to cater to these symptoms to help teams achieve a sustainable pace that can go on indefinitely, treating their agile software development as a marathon, and not mere sprints.

Read, Explore, Evolve

A few good ways to keep a tab on this issue could be team health surveys explicitly asking the question about sustainability to the team.

Bringing up this question in the retrospective could be a good way to trigger the discussion.

Watching out when the discussions in sprint reviews or retrospectives steer too much in the analysis of velocity and its variations. Those could be early signs building up pressure on the team about the work.

REFERENCES

Books

"Mindset: The New Psychology of Success" by Carol Dweck.

'Measure what matters' book by John Doer

'Drive' by Daniel H. Pink

'Coaching Agile Teams' by Lyssa Adkins

'The Lean Startup' by Erik Ries

'Principles of Product development flow' by Don Reinersten

Useful Links

Agile Manifesto - https://agilemanifesto.org/

Principles of Agile Manifesto - https://agilemanifesto.org/principles.html

Scrum Guide - https://www.scrumguides.org/index.html

Lean-Agile Mindset - https://www.scaledagileframework.com/lean-agile-mindset/

The theory behind scrum - Cynefin framework

Extreme Programming – http://www.extremeprogramming.org/

Scaled Agile Framework – https://www.scaledagileframework.com

References

An animated video presenting a summary of book Drive 'Surprising truth behind what motivates us'

Liberating structures - http://www.liberatingstructures.com/

Planning poker video Agile Estimating and Planning: Planning Poker - Mike Cohn

The GE Healthcare empathy and Gemba case study

High performing teams need psychological safety – HBR article

Five keys to a successful google team – Google rework

Speed of trust Videos – Stephen Covey

IMAGE CREDITS

- All cartoons used in this book are from Geek and Poke. The creator of the Geek and Poke cartoon series is Oliver Widder, cartoons are under CC-BY-3.0
- Agile Mindset – The Why before What and How - Image by Arek Socha from Pixabay
- Musings about Mindsets - Image by Mohammed Hassan from Pixabay
- Back to the Basics - Image by DarkWorkX from Pixabay
- Let the Magic begin - Image by S. Hermann & F. Richter from Pixabay
- Make it Transparent - Image by StockSnap from Pixabay and Image by Gerd Altmann from Pixabay
- Openness - Image by Evgeni Tcherkasski from Pixabay
- Courage - Image by Free-Photos from Pixabay
- Feedback Culture - Image by Keith Johnston from Pixabay
- Measure what matters - Image by ImageParty from Pixabay
- Genuinely Collaborate - Image by 272447 from Pixabay
- Self-Organization - Image by Peggy Choucair from Pixabay
- Psychological Safety - Image by TheJohnus from Pixabay
- Trust - Image by RitaE from Pixabay and Image by Alexandra_Koch from Pixabay

Image Credits

- Collective Ownership - Image by Mohammed Hassan from Pixabay
- Respect - Image by argh from Pixabay
- Commitment - Image by Rottonara from Pixabay and Image by Mohammed Hassan from Pixabay
- Life without project managers - Image by Bessi from Pixabay
- Empowerment - Image by matiasarg from Pixabay
- Gemba - Image by Sasin Tipchai from Pixabay
- Customer Centricity - Image by StockSnap from Pixabay
- Working with business - Image by Free-Photos from Pixabay
- Inspect and Adapt - Image by Finn Bjurvoll Hansen from Pixabay
- Focus – being present - Image by Free-Photos from Pixabay
- Timeboxing - Image by Urszula Mazurkiewicz from Pixabay
- Cadence - Image by sam99929 from Pixabay
- Simplicity - Image by friesenliesel from Pixabay
- Prioritization - Image by Elias Sch. from Pixabay
- Continuously Improve - Image by noellepierceromance from Pixabay
- Excellence - Image by Jill Wellington from Pixabay
- Sustainable Development - Image by Annca from Pixabay

www.ingramcontent.com/pod-product-compliance
Lightning Source LLC
Chambersburg PA
CBHW030926180526
45163CB00002B/473